Eight Choices That Can Change a Woman's Life

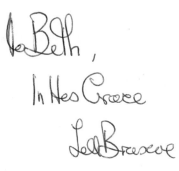

8 Choices That Can Change a Woman's Life

Jill Briscoe

SHAW

WATERBROOK
PRESS

Eight Choices That Can Change A Woman's Life
A SHAW BOOK
PUBLISHED BY WATERBROOK PRESS
2375 Telstar Drive, Suite 160
Colorado Springs, CO 80920
A division of Random House, Inc.

ISBN: 0-87788-208-8

Edited by Miriam Mindeman
Cover design by David LaPlaca
Cover photo by Jeanene Tiner

Library of Congress Cataloging-in-Publication Data

Briscoe, Jill
    Eight choices that can change a woman's life / by Jill Briscoe.
        p. cm.
    Rev. ed. of: De-Baiting the woman trap. c1994
    ISBN 0-87788-208-8
    1. Women—Religious life. 2. Christian life. 3. Briscoe, Jill.
  I. Briscoe, Jill.   De-baiting the woman trap. II. Title.
BV4527.B728   1998
248.8'43—DC21
                                                          98-20193
                                                          CIP

Printed in the United States of America

04 03 02 01 00

10 9 8 7 6 5 4

Contents

Introduction

Our Choices

Our six grandchildren were playing chase, and the condominium rang with the music of their young voices. Five boys and one little girl took turns racing around the traffic pattern of our home, trying to avoid being caught by the others. Once apprehended, the caught one could be a chaser, too. Five little boys had now become the hunters, which left Christy screaming at the top of her lungs and flying into my arms. "Keeping quiet and out of sight might be your best choice right now," I suggested as I entered into the spirit of the game and popped her into the kitchen cupboard alongside the broom. After the boys had a hasty powwow to decide what to do next, I found them in a V-shaped corridor: two of them flattened up against a wall, two others in a stairwell, and one behind the coat rack. They were ready for Christy.

"What are you doing?" I asked them innocently.

"It's a twap for she!" replied one of our three-year-old grandsons seriously (he was sorting his *hers* and *shes*).

Poor little "she," I reflected. From now on, Christy would be facing plenty of "twaps" in this complex world as she grew into a woman desiring to live out authentic Christianity. For—make no mistake about it—the devil lies in wait at the very center of our lives, baiting his traps with all sorts of tempting morsels from his infernal cheese market. I prayed at that moment that whenever Christy faced one of those critical, life-changing choices she would fly for safety as urgently into her heavenly Father's arms as she had into mine!

My desire in this book is to look at some of our most important choices as women, keeping our eyes wide open so we can separate God's way from the more comfortable, even at times deceptively successful, way to live we see all around us. How grateful this particular "church mouse" has been for the godly men and women throughout my life who have helped guide me in many a dangerous moment of choice with their words of warning and wisdom. Above all, I can testify to a loving, caring, compassionate, heavenly Father who has caught me up in his arms so many times and held me until the trouble has passed by. Truly, truly, "God is your refuge, and underneath are the everlasting arms" (Deut. 33:27).

1

To Resist Pain or Use It

The "Me" Trap

Many of us have borne the heartache and sorrow of belonging to a family in which some of those nearest and dearest to us do not know and love the Lord as we do. Even Jesus had that experience! His half-brother James grew up alongside him, misunderstanding his mission and worrying about his "Messiah complex." Everything was probably fine in the family circle until Jesus left home and began his very public ministry. Surely the family began to be concerned about that turn of events!

You can imagine the talk around the supper table as Mary and the children discussed what steps might be taken to persuade Jesus to give up his crusade and come back to the carpenter shop. It was not that the ministry was going badly. On the contrary, things seemed to be going exceptionally well for Jesus and his followers. It was just that there were unsettling rumors about thronging people—the sick, the lepers, the poor—and reports of growing opposition by the rulers in high places. The family must have also worried about the strain of the ministry on Jesus' health.

Perhaps it was the last straw when one day a visitor from Capernaum, the town where Jesus was teaching, brought the information that Jesus and his disciples were so busy they did not even have enough time to eat! (Mark 3:20). It might even have been James who exclaimed, "He is out of his mind!" (v. 21). We do not know who said that, but we do know some family members left their work in Nazareth and traveled thirty miles to Capernaum to try to "take charge of him." When they got there, the crowd was so thick that they could not get near enough to talk to him, so they had to resort to sending him a message. Jesus was told, "Your mother and brothers are outside looking for you" (v. 32). Imagine James's reaction when he learned that Jesus had replied, "Who are my mother and my brothers? . . . Here are my mother and my brothers! Whoever does God's will is my brother and sister and mother" (vv. 33-35). We can only guess at the conversation as the family returned to Nazareth without their mission accomplished, but with Jesus' words ringing in their ears. What could he have meant? Did they not matter to him anymore?

No, James was not in tune with his older half-brother's mission in those turbulent days! However, after Jesus had been crucified and had risen from the dead, James changed his mind about him.

(Imagine how your own mind might change, if your dead brother paid you a visit [1 Cor. 15:7].) Thus we find James, converted and thoroughly convinced of Jesus' divinity, becoming a greatly respected leader of the church in Jerusalem (see Acts 15:13-21; 21:18; Gal. 1:19; 2:9). Concerned about the "twelve tribes" of the dispersion, he wrote the Jewish Christians a letter.

James's consuming passion was authentic Christianity. He wanted to see the followers of Christ live like Christ and die like Christ. In a world where myriad religious philosophers vied for men's minds, James urged believers to act according to their beliefs, practice what they preached, and refuse to be redundant.

James believed that real religion—transparent, winsome, clean, exciting, and trustworthy—must be practiced daily if an unbelieving world was to take the Christian message seriously. Such faith, he warned, was bound to be challenged. Darkness cannot abide light, error hisses at truth, corruption tries to bury resurrection life. Being a disciple of Jesus Christ was not for sissies. Jesus, James's half-brother, had used vivid imagery to warn his followers what lay ahead. He had talked about sending them out as "sheep among wolves," where devils and demons would do their worst and the prince of all evil, Satan himself, would surely treat the Master's servants as badly as the Master himself was treated. This was no time to be "me"-centered. Rather, James urged the believers to be "he"-centered—to focus on Jesus.

In James's day, church leaders led, Christians bled, and darkness fled as the infant church fought the devil bravely. And the blood of martyrs nourished the seed of the church. No doubt, even in such a time as this, while moral failure and other sins among the rulers of the church were unthinkable, they surely happened. But we might wonder how the state of church leadership then compares with our leadership today. At the end of our twentieth century, we see church leaders as prominent as James using all modern means, including television, to tell the old, old story in a new, new way. Unfortunately, all too often we have watched from thousands of armchairs as these modern versions of James have shocked us by exposing their prime sins on prime time! Can you imagine what an impact there would have been on the early church if Peter had confessed to adultery, Nathaniel to mishandling of funds, or Mary and Martha to hiring an illegal alien? In James's day, as persecution purified the church, temptation and trials served mainly as a dark backdrop that highlighted the golden deeds of sinners who became saints in a hurry.

When James wrote his letter, Christians were everywhere. Every day they multiplied. Unsaved people had a chance to work the plow with Christ's followers. They could daily collect water from the well or ride to market with genuine believers. It was not long till everyone seemed to know someone who was talking about Jesus of Nazareth. As the world's people heard the gospel and watched the early church in action, thousands found Christ.

One of the problems with our world, as compared to James's world, centers around the enhanced visibility of leaders without Christian integrity and the scarcity of lively laity! Many people probably equate a born-again, evangelical Christian with the one or two prominent TV personalities they have become accustomed to seeing on the tube. The highly visible fall—and crash—of some of those well-known televangelists into the moral abyss has too frequently served to make ordinary Christians objects of ridicule rather than lights in a dark world.

A friend of mine attended a PTA meeting where she struck up a conversation with a young mother. In the course of their talk, my friend spoke quite naturally about her faith and about how Christ had been a personal help and comfort to her. The young mother listened with fascination and wanted to know more. "You're the first born-again person I've met who isn't on TV," she said. That's scary!

The cynicism that is "out there" concerning authentic Christianity was brought home to me personally one day when I received a call from a viewer who had been watching our church TV program and who bluntly asked me, "Is Briscoe genuine?"

I dislike anyone calling my husband "Briscoe," but I needed to answer civilly. "I live with him," I replied, "and the answer is yes!" We had a good talk after that, with the caller explaining that he liked to watch my husband, but had been so disillusioned by other TV preachers messing up that he had become somewhat of a cynic about so-called religious people.

I could not blame him—but I was able to encourage the caller to "watch on," pointing out that if he found one doctor who was a quack, it probably would not deter him from using the service of other members of the health profession! Putting the phone down, I thought of James's letter and imagined how horrified he would have been to receive such a phone call. How is it, he would have asked, that so many Christians have fallen into such a "me" trap? Today, others ask, "How can so many believers be so much like soft-serve ice cream—light on nutrients and with so little substance? Perhaps we need to read James's letter regularly, just to keep sharp and prevent a blunted conscience.

The devil baits his "me" traps with tempting, promising, "easy" cheese, and we church mice are taken off guard, believing we have an inalienable right to be happy, healthy, and loved by the world at large and the church in particular. We rudely slam the door in trouble's face and race back to our flowery beds of ease, horrified at the specter of hardship. We are convinced that being a favored child of God brings exemption from the pain that others experience. James actually suggests we should welcome such intrusions as friends and not regard them as enemies, going so far as to tell us to count such trials as pure joy! (1:2).

Satan hopes the narcissistic tenor of the world around us will mold our minds and our manners to match the thinking and actions of people who do not know the Lord and his ways. Because the whole human race outside of Christ has already been ambushed into the "me" trap, their total way of life appears to be an effort to avoid pain and embrace pleasure. With that outlook, if we have a headache, we dive for the aspirin; if we do not like our job (or our spouse), we change it or him. If we visit a family with a new baby, we take presents for the baby and all the other kids, in case they might feel bad at being overlooked.

This is not to say that Christians should be masochists! I do not believe we are to place ourselves in harm's way, but we can certainly expect a few uninvited visits from trouble. Unbidden pain can be a friend, triggering healthy reactions, helping us to avoid danger, or acting as an early warning system. Philip Yancey in his book *Where Is God When It Hurts?* (Zondervan, 1977) says that "not only is pain useful as a warning, it may also be an essential dimension in our richest experiences." He adds that this may seem odd to the modern Christian mind which has been trapped into thinking that "pain is the antithesis of pleasure."

Paul, commenting on the questions that crowd into our minds when crisis comes calling, says, "God sometimes uses sorrow in our lives to help us turn away from sin and seek eternal life" (2 Cor. 7:10, TLB). This was certainly the case for me. God once used a pain in my stomach to get me into a hospital—but more importantly to get me into heaven! I was a busy, happy student, minding my own business and having a good time. Then came the stomachache that would not go away. In the end the ambulance came and whisked me off to be prodded and poked, X-rayed and examined. It was a full week and a half before the medical staff came up with some answers. During that time—my first in a hospital—I had come to see sorrow up close. The face of a mother keeping watch over her dying teenage daughter. The elderly lady always alone, even when we all had visitors at our bedsides. The woman who lost her father while she was immobilized after surgery and so could not attend the funeral. Lots of pain, lots of tears, lots of sorrow.

Yet God used my own personal pain to help me "turn away from sin and seek eternal life." Pain prepared me (in a way pleasure could never have done) to consider the issues of life and death and to decide for Jesus Christ. Once I had become a Christian, I discovered that sorrow was not to be feared but rather endured with hope and expectancy that God would use it to visit and bless my life.

Traveling around the world as I do, I have been struck with the different attitudes toward suffering that I have encountered. As someone has said, "In the West we cry, 'God, get this trouble off my back,' whereas Christians in the East have been accustomed to cry out instead, 'God, strengthen my back to bear it!'" If, as women reflecting our culture, we claim the right to be pain-free and pleasure-satiated, we will find ourselves caught tightly in a misery-me snare, notwithstanding our Christian faith.

Erma Bombeck (one of my favorite prophetesses), commented wisely in a newspaper column I clipped about fifteen years ago:

> During the last year I have dissected my marriage, examined my motives for buying, interpreted my fantasies, come to grips with midlife, found inner peace, outer flab, charted my astrological stars, become my best and only friend. I have brought order to my life, meditated, given up guilt, adjusted to the new morality, and spent every living hour understanding me, interpreting me, and loving me. And . . . you know what? I am bored to death of me.

The results of being ego-centric instead of Christo-centric are boredom, nonfulfillment, and a bad self-image. It stands to reason that God's creatures, living in God's world, sustained by God, intended by God to live for God, will be pretty miserable divorced from God.

In his book entitled *The Great Divorce,* C. S. Lewis wrote about sin coming between God and humanity. He believed that the remarriage of God and man through Christ's death and resurrection brought reconciliation between the divorced parties. Yet some Christians seem to flirt with the world for the rest of their lives, thus falling into the "me" trap and putting their relationship with God on hold.

God says that reconnection with him will never be boring, for at his right hand are "eternal pleasures" (Ps. 16:11). This wonderful God-connection is totally fulfilling. Those who have experienced this relationship will tell you that its pleasures will far outweigh any transitory pain.

How, then, do we get out of the "me" trap? We can start by asking the Lord to lift the steel spring and set us free. Christ has the strength to not only liberate us but also keep us free! But first we have to recognize that we have made the choice to follow Satan's deception, to eat the cheese he offers. We can start by looking at our reaction to suffering. If we ask angrily, "What is this trouble doing in my life?" we have not realized that the trouble we are suffering is acceptable to the Lord and therefore should be acceptable to us. If we continue angrily fighting against what God has allowed, we are well trapped into an attitude of mind that can only add to the trouble that has already invaded our lives!

When the troubles in Bosnia were at their height, Gary Cox, a Christian worker helping relief agencies with refugees in the camps in Serbia, wrote a report in which he demonstrated that the troubles in that war-torn corner of Europe were introducing people to life and liberty of an altogether different kind than that sought by the warring factions. "It's not just our stomachs that are hungry but also our hearts," is one comment he recorded from a Serbian refugee whose Muslim husband was a prisoner of war. A Serbian evangelist is quoted as saying, "Some Serbian refugees even express joy at losing everything but finding Jesus." The report tells of pastors with waiting lists of new believers requesting baptism. Apparently, though many are skeptical about lasting political solutions to the region's problems, there is considerable interest in the promise of peace with God! (*Evangelism Today*, #254, June 1993).

C. S. Lewis wrote in *The Problem of Pain*, "God whispers to us in our pleasures, speaks in our conscience, but shouts in our pains; it is his megaphone to rouse a deaf world." But our society has convinced us—Christians and non-Christians alike—that we will be content only if we can avoid trouble. Some of the most discontented women I know have the most trouble-free lives! On the other hand, a paraplegic woman named Joni Erickson has testified, "My paralysis has drawn me close to God and given a spiritual healing which I wouldn't trade for a hundred active years on my feet!" How could she say that? Because the God of grace has visited her world of suffering, and He and she have become the best of friends! It was trouble that introduced Joni to God.

A few years ago, our church invited Joni to speak to our community. The night before we were to have the meeting, Joni and her caregivers stayed in a local hotel. I called to take her to the meeting the next morning. She had a room on the top floor, and we waited for the elevator along with quite a large group of business people. "What are you going to speak about?" I asked Joni, drawing a few curious glances.

"Grace," she replied, "but I'm going to sing first." By now we were all crowded around her wheelchair in the elevator. As clear as a bell, Joni began to practice. Seemingly oblivious of the people locked into the experience, Joni sang "Amazing Grace" right through! I looked around the elevator. Some folk were staring at the ceiling, but most of the men and women were staring at "grace" personified. They saw a beautiful woman paralyzed from the neck down, but more whole than most of us in that small box with our bodies in good working order. There were not a few tears as we reached the ground floor and went on our way.

How can you be content in a refugee camp with your husband a prisoner of war? How can you be content in a wheelchair? Only by knowing the God of grace, who sent Jesus to be the Prince of Peace and who can give us the peace which "transcends all understanding" (Phil. 4:7). Anyone can understand having peace of heart when all is well, but it "transcends understanding" when you experience peace in the midst of disaster!

And there are so many disasters today! I often find myself listening to a litany of trouble detailed and recounted by Christian brothers and sisters who are in an immense amount of pain. I marvel at the endurance and perseverance of so many who go through those deep, dark tunnels of affliction. They do not have it easy. But they do have it licked! Trouble is beating down on them, but they are beating trouble! Christ does that for them, and Christ can do that for all of us. What is more, these people talk of the blessings these troubles have brought along in their train.

And that is exactly what James was talking about in his letter. He said in James 1:2-3, "When all kind of trials and temptations crowd into your lives . . . don't resent them as intruders, but welcome them as friends" (PHILLIPS). Friends bring blessings into our lives. When some missionary friends of ours had their house broken into for the third time and their belongings stolen, they "joyfully accepted the confiscation of [their] property" (Heb. 10:34). They recognized a friend! If we can only realize that such things happen to us to test our faith and produce in us the quality of endurance that helps us to become spiritually mature, we will find a huge measure of comfort in that.

You may be asking, "Maturity for what?" Maturity so you are ready for anything! Some of us are ready for nothing very much, but James says, "When the way is rough, your patience has a chance to grow. So let it grow, and don't try to squirm out of your problems. For when your patience is finally in full bloom, then you will be ready for anything, strong in character, full and complete" (James 1:3-4, TLB). Not only can trouble make us mature in the sense that we are ready for anything; it can also make us ready for God. When do we most urgently seek the Almighty? I suspect it is when trouble intrudes itself into our peaceful little lives and we need his guidance and wisdom.

A traveler reading a book on a train noticed a friendly little girl playing around the seats, talking to the other passengers and showing them her toys.

The traveler put down his book and exchanged a few words with her, wondering whom she belonged to. She seemed perfectly at ease with everyone, so it was hard to tell. Suddenly the train entered a long, dark tunnel, and the lights flickered. The traveler smiled when the little girl darted toward a lady sitting at the end of the carriage and flung herself into her arms. There was no doubt now whom she belonged to!

The world constantly watches those of us who love Jesus. Perhaps they wonder whom we belong to. While everything is going well, it may be hard to tell. But let us enter a long, dark tunnel, and there will be absolutely no doubt. They will watch us dive into the arms of God, and then they will know! Just as surely as suffering gets us ready for him, it also alerts a watching world to a source of help they know nothing about. There are many travelers on the train of life who need to see that happen.

How can we possibly experience peace without battle, joy without sorrow, or wisdom without problems that have to be solved? We cannot know one without the other. Even more important, however, we can know in reality a love that will not let us go in the midst of the trouble.

> O Love that will not let me go,
> I rest my weary soul in thee;
> I give thee back the life I owe,
> That in thine ocean depths its flow
> May richer, fuller be.
>
> O Light that followest all my way,
> I yield my flickering torch to thee;
> My heart restores its borrowed ray,

That in thy sunshine's blaze its day
May brighter, fairer be.

O Joy that seekest me through pain
I cannot close my heart to thee;
I trace the rainbow through the rain,
And feel the promise is not vain
That morn shall tearless be.

O Cross that liftest up my head,
I dare not ask to fly from thee;
I lay in dust life's glory dead,
And from the ground there blossoms red
Life that shall endless be.

—George Matheson, 1882

The apostle Paul wrote that problems and trials help us to experience the presence of a God who is love and who develops perseverance in us as we persevere. And patience develops strong character in us and helps us trust God more each time we use it until finally our hope and faith are strong and steady (Rom. 5:3-4, TLB). Phillips renders this passage, "We can be full of joy here and now even in our trials and troubles. *Taken in the right spirit* these things will give us patient endurance" (italics added). Such a good experience with suffering demands a sharing of the secret! This way we can begin to serve others who are also in trouble.

You may well ask, "How do I know who will need my help?" James drew up a catalog of needy people for us, in case we asked that question. First he talks about "the brother in humble circumstances" (1:9). There are many of those in our world. But if you link yourself up with a reputable Christian relief organization such as World Relief (450 E. Gundersen Dr., Carol Stream, IL 60188) that serves the church in trouble worldwide, you will be sent pictures of your brothers and sisters in the humblest of circumstances and shown how to serve them on a practical level. James also talks about the person "who perseveres under trial (1:12). You do not have to look to the Third and Fourth Worlds to find one of these. They live next door, work in your office, serve you in the grocery store!

One day while grocery shopping, I heard some talk about my next-door neighbor. It was casual scuttlebutt, but it alerted me to the fact that my neighbor's husband had just walked out on her. Here was a middle-aged woman whose husband had left her for a younger model! Though I did not know this neighbor, I plucked up enough courage to make an apple pie, walk over the back lawn separating our houses, knock on her door, and say, "I've heard what happened. You're in trouble, and I'm so sorry. Can I help?" The lady practically grabbed me by the lapels and pulled me inside the house.

James also talks about the person in shabby clothes (2:2), the hungry and homeless (2:15), orphans and widows (1:27), and underpaid workers (5:4). These are all people we walk past (or over) in the train stations and downtown in any metropolis, or find ourselves sitting next to in the church pew on any given Sunday. We will have eyes to see them only if we choose to live in a serving, not a self-serving, mode.

As a busy young mother of three preschool children, I was once invited to go to downtown Manchester, England, to see what some local Christians were doing about some needy street kids. At first I did not feel I had the necessary time, energy, or inclination at the end of my hectic day. But my friend persuaded me to get a sitter and go. (After all, I got sitters for other things!)

If ever I met need on my doorstep, it was that night. These young people fitted James's descriptions perfectly. They were wearing ragged clothes; they were homeless, orphaned, or totally destitute. I knew it was up to me to get involved. But what about our own kids? We were living on a very small salary. If I began to spend time with other people's children, what would happen to mine? Yet was not the whole point of living Christianity to be living like Christ lived? He *always* extended himself for people in trouble, and he never had much money or time either! What I chose to do with this opportunity depended on whether or not I was in the "me" trap. James must have had his older half-brother in mind when he urged his readers to go beyond themselves and serve others in need.

The woman who "just says no" to the temptation of choosing selfishness over service will drop into bed at night and know she has not had one solitary minute to think about herself. Anyone who not only says no to an egocentric lifestyle but also welcomes trouble—not as an intruder, but as a friend—will realize that trouble trains us (as nothing else can do) to empathize with and serve troubled people.

"But you can't just start talking to strangers," some object. Certainly we can get into problems if we are reckless. But there are so many casual acquaintances within our circle of influence that we can safely start precisely in the setting where God has placed us.

Half the battle is won by choosing to look *out* instead of focusing always inside ourselves. Being Christ-centered means being people-centered. If we go out into our day determined to be a blessing, our eyes will be searching for someone to bless, and we will be smiling! In fact, that is exactly where you can start. Just keep smiling! I have found that such a simple thing has opened many a conversation with people in need. There are so few smiles out there—perhaps because for many people there seems nothing much to smile about! Last week I set off on a trip and smiled my way to my destination. It was wonderful! "Thank you," I said enthusiastically to the pilot and stewardess as I bid them a dutiful goodbye at the door of the plane. (I noticed that few others acknowledged their departure graciously.) The pilot looked shocked—and grateful. I smiled at the taxi driver, the receptionist at the hotel, and the porter who brought my bags upstairs. "Have a good day," I said, tipping him generously.

"I'll try, Miss," he said hesitantly.

"Not a good day for you?" I inquired gently.

"No, Miss," he said, "but I'm glad it's a good one for you."

"It isn't so good on the outside," I confided, "but it is on the inside." Here was a chance to smile and give him a booklet explaining what I meant. He smiled back and took it! Of course, I had been tempted to think exclusively about getting settled in—putting my feet up for a brief respite, watching TV, being me-centered. But James had told me not to have this mindset! It is not always easy to avoid this, especially when you have a natural tendency to pamper yourself!

Not long ago, I fell into bed exhausted after a busy week of travel and ministry. Feeling a little sorry for myself, I looked at my husband for a bit of sympathy. He merely grinned at me and asked cheerfully, "Are you feeling 'weary with well doing'?" (Gal. 6:9, KJV).

"Yes," I replied rather pathetically.

"It's a great feeling, isn't it?" he commented, happily returning to his book.

I lay there thinking about that, and after a bit I had to admit he was right.

Peter tells us, "Do not be surprised at the painful trial you are suffering, as though something strange were happening to you" (1 Pet. 4:12). Yet, all too often, those of us caught firmly in the "me" trap react exactly like that! Even when a little spark of sorrow falls into our lap, we moan, "How strange that this should happen to someone as nice as me! I feel hurt." Like Miss Piggy, we cry *"Moi?* How could God let this happen to *moi?"* Trouble, however, can actually make us a whole lot more others-conscious and lead us to choose Christian social action. *The Living Bible* talks about our being "bewildered" when trouble comes, even though "this is no strange, unusual thing." It is indeed not unusual for Christian faith to bring with it opportunities to grow the flowers of perseverance in our lives—to become "partners with Christ in his suffering" (1 Pet. 4:13, TLB).

One long-ago day I was busy mothering our three lively toddlers as my husband came home from work and said, "The boss has told me he wants me to go to the States for a time and do some preaching and teaching."

I was excited. "What an opportunity," I responded. "When are you going and for how long?"

I expected him to say, "In a month or so and for

just a couple of weeks." Instead he replied, "Next month and for twelve weeks."

I stopped mopping up children and gazed at him dumbstruck. I wanted to cry out, "What about me? How can you go and leave me with three kids for so long? It isn't fair." I felt the "me" trap snap painfully over my heart, so tightly I could hardly breathe. The next few weeks I struggled to free myself from the self-pity and panic that awaited me as I woke up every morning. How could I escape? Who could change my feelings? As I turned to God's Word, I read, "And he died for all, that those who live should no longer live for themselves but for him who died for them and was raised again" (2 Cor. 5:15). I realized that God was not asking me to do this lonely thing primarily for my husband, but for *him!* What is more, it was for him who died for me! Jesus left his family for the sake of *my* family. He knew all about loneliness. Now our family could do something for him. And not only could I live for him who died for me, I could live out this coming period of separation from Stuart in the power of the risen Christ, for as the apostle Paul had reminded me, it was for him who died *and was raised again.* I knew there was no other way. Choosing in God's power to accept that particular trial (which incidentally was followed by years of long separations) gave me space and time to take care of a lot of the problem people listed in James's catalog. For me, sorrow certainly led to service!

Who could have guessed I would start a play school in the little town nearby—a school that would end up ministering to hundreds of children, the handicapped among them? How could I have known the future and seen the skills with youth evangelism I would acquire in those lonely years, skills that perhaps would never have been discovered if my husband had stayed home? And who could possibly have known I would learn to use a pen and paper and write poems, Bible books, plays, and children's literature in my unasked-for and at first unwelcomed "space"? Yes, for me, sorrow led to service. The school of sorrow is not one any of us willingly enrolls in, but once we have completed a semester or two, we are glad we had the benefit of its instructors.

How can you resist the temptation to succumb to the "me" trap? First of all, remember that the devil is neither original nor creative. His devices do not change. The same old egocentric deceptions will appear throughout everyone's short life, and we must all learn to recognize them.

Second, be on special alert when, in God's will, trouble comes calling. These will be special moments when we are particularly susceptible to electing self-preservation above all other considerations. Try to welcome these trials, as James calls them, as friends rather than intruders. Remember that friends can make us strong and ready for anything.

Third, run to God often, and know what to do when you get there. Be familiar enough with Scripture so you know where help can be found in its pages. Learn to pray, and try not to panic.

Finally, be aware that people are watching how you, a Christian, respond to trouble. Let them see you receive God's comfort, and then let them watch you pass on that comfort to others in need. In other words, let them observe how sorrow leads you to service rather than to self-pity.

Christ never allowed himself to fall into the "me" trap, and he can lend us the inner wisdom to know how to follow his example. All we have to do is ask. For, "If any of you is lacking in wisdom, ask God, who gives to all generously and ungrudgingly, and it will be given you" (James 1:5).

We are little church mice,
and the devil sets a trap
For all unwary Christians
he sees are in a flap.
He loves to stir up trouble
and send pain into our life.
He tempts us to go for "easy cheese"
and bypass all the strife.
But God says that's a "me" trap,
and we're not to be surprised
When pain and trouble
call on us, but rather recognize
That joy awaits the one who'll say,
"Come in now, little trouble.
If you make me like Christ my Lord,
the blessing will be double!"
So focus first on God himself;
be practical in deed.
And as you tell your world of Christ,
you'll find he'll meet your need!

—J.B.

Study Guide: The "Me" Trap
For Personal Growth and/or
Group Discussion

1. There are two motivational and lifestyle extremes: *5 minutes*

   (a) To avoid pain and embrace pleasure
   (b) To avoid pleasure and embrace pain

   Where is the balance for the Christian? Discuss.

2. Read 2 Corinthians 7:8-11. Can you identify with what Paul says in this passage?   *15 minutes*

   (a) Share your own experience of God that came through sorrow.
   (b) Share a lesson you learned about patience and/or endurance through trouble.

3. In the following passages, James speaks of many people who need help. List the counterparts to these people in our society.
   10 minutes

James 1:9	James 2:13
James 1:12	James 5:3-4
James 1:27	James 5:14
James 2:2	James 5:20

4. Which of these people are you drawn to and

why? Think of how you could serve them. (Brainstorm and share ideas.) *10 minutes*

Prayer Time *10 minutes*

1. Reread Erma Bombeck's words on page 16. Do you know people like this? Pray for them.

2. Pray for any Christians you know who are in trouble and are not coping very well.

3. Pray for the homeless, the poor, the persecuted, and others in need.

4. Pray for yourself.

2

To Gather Wealth or Gather Grace

The Money Trap

In his book *Celebration of Discipline,* Richard Foster says,

> The modern hero is the poor boy who purposely becomes rich, rather than the rich boy who voluntarily becomes poor! Hoarding we call prudence, greed we call industry. Owning is an obsession in our culture. We are all fascinated with the lives of the rich and famous. Wealth we are told is the benchmark of achievement. It does not seem to be a question of how much character you have—but rather how much cash!

Shortly after I came to faith while a student, I was given a book about the life of C. T. Studd, a brilliant Cambridge student who had played cricket for England and covered himself with glory. Studd came from an extremely wealthy home and materially lacked nothing. Then he came to Christ—a Christ who captured his heart, forgave his sins, and gave him a passion to share both his faith and his wealth. That focus never diminished. After joining a small group of like-minded Cambridge men, who came to be known as the Cambridge Seven, and giving away his entire inheritance, Studd took off for China with this intrepid group of young idealists to win souls for Christ.

In a small booklet called "The Chocolate Soldier," Studd wrote: "Some like to live within the sound of church or chapel bell, I want to run a rescue shop within a yard of hell." I was absolutely captivated as I read this man's story. As far as I was concerned, here was a hero indeed. He went to China, to India, and eventually to the heart of Africa, making inroads for the gospel where Christ's name had never before been heard. He was tough, yet he was tender, and he loved God with such a passion that I caught the fire in his bones and can truly say, "I have never been the same since!"

Coming from a moderately well-off family myself (though certainly not nearly as wealthy as Studd's was), I found that this book struck a needed note for me right at the start of my Christian life. His testimony has done more to save me from falling into the money trap than any sermon ever could! Here was a hero very different from those I had been accustomed to. Before my conversion, I used to gawk at the "goggle box" (as we called it), tuning in to the antics of Hollywood idols, the elite European *nouveau riche* at Mediterranean resorts, or the high-fashion models on the catwalks of London or Paris showrooms. I had seen money as the key to the good and beautiful life—the fun life. But now I had new eyes to see, new ears to hear, and a new heart to feel the Lord's feelings about the pounds, shillings, and pence that had once seemed to glitter and glow so invitingly before me. In the words of a favorite hymn of mine:

> Heaven above is softer blue,
> Earth around is sweeter green!
> Something lives in every hue,
> Christless eyes have never seen:
> Birds with gladder songs o'er-flow,
> Flow'rs with deeper beauties shine,
> Since I know, as now I know,
> I am his, and he is mine.
> —George Wade Robinson

My father had begun his very successful business career by going from house to house asking people if they wanted their bicycles or cars fixed. Vowing he would never work for anyone but himself, he began his business in his garage and ended up with a large, privately owned motorcar company in the north of England. Money had not come easily, but it *had* come, and I owed my education, vacations abroad, sports training, and lovely home environment—in fact, all a young, post-World War II woman would want—to my father's hard-won prosperity. At the same time, I observed up close that it is one thing to make it—another thing to keep it. I watched the care lines appear early on my father's face and bouts of depression haunt him.

I began to understand that wealth is relative, anyway. Keeping up with the Joneses in your neighborhood may not mean keeping up with the Joneses in the next classier, brassier subdivision. One edition of Webster's defines wealth as "a large amount of something valuable ... abundance ... affluence." Compared to a newly arrived immigrant, our family was fabulously wealthy, but in terms of people who lived in impressive country mansions, we were only moderately well-off. I also observed that we hardly ever compared ourselves with the immigrant, but rather with the richer "hero" we heard about. We were prey to that feeling that if there is someone richer than you around, then you are not yet quite rich enough—a disease that someone has aptly called "affluenza"!

The wonder of accumulated wealth included connotations of influence in the community, lavish spending, ostentation, luxury, and sumptuous living. Certainly one could be duped into thinking that happiness, power, kingdoms, and empires were all part of the package, and all necessary for living a normal, satisfying life.

Yet one definition of *rich* is: "the general word to describe one who has more money or income-producing property than is necessary to satisfy his normal needs." And there is the trap! We are convinced we need more because we still have "needs" to meet and are conned into thinking that money can buy us the happiness that seems just out of our grasp. Which of us reading this is indeed rich according to that definition? Surely, nearly all of us.

But the devil baits the money trap with greed, and church mice are just as likely as nonbelievers to get more than their whiskers caught in this one!

The greed-need tempts all of us to strive to catch up to and live up to the particular family of Joneses living beyond our particular garden fence. The problem is that little something inside every one of us that is never satisfied with merely having its needs met—it wants its wants to be met, too! If we set about getting our *wants* met, we will find ourselves wanting more than the "enough" that meets our needs. In fact, the more we get, the more we want. Webster's says that greed is "an excessive desire for getting or having (especially wealth); a desire for more than one needs or deserves; avarice." It expands this definition further: "Wanting or taking all that one can get with no thought of others' needs." Greed is a "getting" obsession—a religion all of its own, leading to idolatry.

This greed-need is part of every human heart, part of our "earthly nature" (Col. 3:5). Every single human being is born with a greedy heart. What, for example, is usually the first word articulated by a toddler in respect to his worldly goods, namely toys? *Mine!*

I have a vivid picture of my little girl, age three, gathering up her favorite toys, books, and even clothes into the small circle of her arms and carrying them protectively all over the house. You see, Judy had two brothers, one older and one younger! I can still see her little frowning face, telling me she was worried because she could not carry all her belongings to safety. And which of us has not participated in a Christmas party where children are present and watched them open all their gifts, only to ask for *more?*

We are born with this propensity. It comes from Eve, the mother of us all. Satan began to set up the money trap before there ever was any of the green stuff. He did not tempt Eve with a fortune but with a piece of fruit. The "substance" was not the issue, for God had provided everything she could possibly require. The issue was the desire to possess for herself the thing that was forbidden— off limits. When Satan put the idea into Eve's head that she needed that object to make her happy, she transferred her attention and her love away from God and onto the object of temptation. She wanted more! If we are loving and obeying God and are focused on him, we will find that he will be all that we need, and we will tell Satan so. I have met many people around the world who through life's hardships have been stripped of everything this world holds dear, yet who possess God's treasure in the person of Christ. I have heard them testify again and again that when Jesus is all they have, Jesus is all they want!

The Bible says that greed is idolatry, and Jesus condemns *mammon* (the Aramaic term for "wealth") as a rival god: "No servant can serve two masters. Either he will hate the one and love the other, or he will be devoted to the one and despise the other. You cannot serve both God and Money" (Luke 16:13). If greed-need is our god, we will do whatever he tells us to do. We will, however, find the greed god an unrelenting deity. There are no lasting returns. We will simply end up craving things we neither need nor enjoy, once we have obtained them. Are we hooked on having? Arthur Gish comments in *Beyond the Rat Race,* "We buy things we do not want to impress people we do not like." Yet impress them we do! That is part of the trap, for greed attracts its own kind. A greedy person has no trouble finding greedy friends.

Think of the story Jesus told about the prodigal son who went to his father, hands outstretched, saying, "Gimme, gimme, gimme" (see Luke 15: 11-31). The father complied, giving his son the part of his inheritance due him, whereupon he took off to the big city to spend it all in wild living. That sort of wealth attracts fair-weather friends. As the writer of Ecclesiastes puts it, "As goods increase, so do those who consume them" (Eccles. 5:11). But the prodigal found that when the money was all gone, no one stayed around to give him anything. Greed becomes a demanding taskmaster, producing an addiction that can lead us to self-destruction.

The young man in Jesus' story ended up in a pigpen. Quite a disastrous situation for a true-blue Jew like him, especially since observant Jews do not even eat pig meat! In other words, he found himself a long way from his family roots, his spiritual inheritance. That is what the greed-need can do to any of us. Fortunately, the experience had a salutary effect on the prodigal. First he came to himself; then he came to his father and begged forgiveness. He realized that true wealth lay in an altogether different direction than the one he had been heading in. True wealth is family, love, forgiveness, and a godly heritage. After Jesus had finished telling his story of the prodigal son, a few in the crowd who were poor would be comforted to know that though they were poor as far as this world's goods were concerned, they were wealthy as God counted wealth.

In the end, the devil does not really care what we crave as long as we crave it. We can be hungry for money, power, or sex, but we can be just as hungry for beauty aids, books, CD's, or outlet shopping! The devil's only concern is that he catch us firmly in his "things" trap. Once he sees we have developed an unhealthy addiction to acquiring things, he works on our need to keep safe those things we possess. He is intent on our hoarding or storing up our acquired wealth. Then the real headache begins! The panic attacks start, the anxiety fits catch us by surprise. Solomon, the richest man of his time, said, "The abundance of a rich man permits him no sleep. I have seen a grievous evil under the sun: wealth hoarded to the harm of its owner" (Eccles. 5:12-13). We can find ourselves spending an incredible amount of time and money protecting and keeping what we have, even when it leads to our own hurt.

James talks about this in his letter (5:1-6). He says that greedy, selfish persons who hoard become bankrupt inside. They might well have a big bank balance, but there is no personal balance whatsoever inside their soul—only the sickening sensation of something terribly askew and "corroded."

Paul, in writing to the Corinthians, cautions against gorging on such greed and becoming "engrossed" with the things of the world. He reminds them and us that "the time is short. . . . Those who buy something [should buy it] as if it were not theirs to keep. . . . For this world in its present form is passing away" (1 Cor. 7:29-31). How can we know if we are firmly caught in the money trap?

When we are living as though that which is material is permanent and that which is permanent is immaterial!

Jesus warned, "Take care! Be on your guard against all kinds of greed; for one's life does not consist in the abundance of possessions" (Luke 12:15, NRSV). In other words, life is more than money and the things we acquire. In a pointed parable (a heavenly story with an earthly meaning) Jesus told of a rich man who said to himself, "You have plenty of good things laid up for many years. Take life easy; eat, drink and be merry" (Luke 12:19). God commented succinctly that the man was a fool, for that very night his life would be taken from him. Then the Lord asked, "Who will get what you have prepared for yourself?" (v. 20). The fool learned very late that you can't take it with you!

I once heard a story about a rich man who owned a lot of property. He lived in a mansion on a hill overlooking his land holdings. He was not a believer, but he had a faithful Christian gardener who prayed for his master diligently. One night the servant, "Honest John" as he was known, had a troublesome dream in which a voice said that the richest man in the valley would die at the stroke of midnight. Wakened by the dream, he was so convinced his master was about to be ushered into eternity that he determined to pluck up his courage and talk to him about it. This he did, only to be met by a hearty laugh, a pat on the shoulder, and a kindly smile as his master replied, "Why, Honest John, you needn't be worried about me—though I appreciate the kind thoughts. You'd better be looking after your own health problems," he suggested.

"Didn't you have some blood pressure problems a while back? I'll be fine, so just go on back to work now."

Amused at the gardener's irrational notion, but still a little concerned, the richest man in the valley picked up the phone to call his doctor. "Would you like to come over tonight and play a game of cards with me about ten o'clock?" he asked. The doctor thought the late hour a bit strange but complied, and as the time approached midnight, he noticed his host casting surreptitious glances at the clock. "Anything wrong?" the doctor inquired.

"No, nothing at all," the richest man in the valley replied hastily, chiding himself for allowing the gardener to get to him with his silly, religious nonsense. He had always thought that people like John, people who had been "born again," whatever that meant, were a little weird with their belief in the Bible and their visions and dreams.

The clock struck midnight, and the richest man in the valley found himself counting along. He was annoyed with himself for feeling relieved when the chiming was through and he was none the worse! Saying good-bye to his doctor friend, he went upstairs to bed. At twelve-thirty the doorbell rang, and without thinking the rich man ran down the stairs to open the door. He found a young girl crying on the doorstep. "Who are you?" he asked. "And what do you want?"

"I just came to tell you, sir," she sobbed, "that tonight at midnight my father died."

"And who is your father?" asked the surprised man.

"Honest John is his name," she replied. "The richest man in the valley!"

And so John was! Christ was this humble gardener's treasure, as he is ours. He comes into our lives and makes us richer than our wildest dreams. What is more, this heavenly wealth is such that "moth and rust do not destroy, and . . . thieves do not break in and steal" (Matt. 6:20).

In England there is an interesting little thing that happens when someone dies. After probate in court, the deceased's estate—how much he or she is leaving and to whom—appears in the local paper. One day Stuart's father was reading the *Westmorland Gazette*. My father-in-law called to his wife, who was busy in the kitchen, "That's interesting. Mrs. Jones died."

"Oh, really?" Stuart's mother replied. "How much did she leave?"

"Everything," said my father-in-law adroitly! We all chuckled. It was indeed true. As Job put it, "Naked I came from my mother's womb, and naked I will depart" (Job 1:21). Paul said about the same thing: "We brought nothing into the world, and we can take nothing out of it" (1 Tim. 6:7). James spoke to the church of his day and addressed the greed-need. As he tried to warn them (and us) about the money trap, he pointed out that it is not a question of how many accumulated goods one has that matters, but one's attitude toward them. We and our wealth "will soon be gone" (1:10, TLB).

God certainly trusts some of his children with a great deal of material wealth! It is God's gift. Moses reminded the children of Israel, "It is he who gives you the ability to produce wealth" (Deut. 8:18). But though God entrusts only a few of his children with material wealth, he trusts all of his children with spiritual wealth! And we do well to remember that these riches were bestowed at so very great a cost. Someone has defined the grace of God with an acrostic: **G**od's **R**iches **A**t **C**hrist's **E**xpense. The Holy Spirit makes spiritual millionaires out of all who possess him. It is as we discover our spiritual inheritance as children of the King that we get a handle on managing our material wealth and being content with it, however little or much it may be.

One of the things we discover as we know Christ and increasingly experience his life in us is a growing spirit of generosity: a willingness to share. Thinking again of our three-year-old Judy—trying to survive as the middle child and endeavoring to carry all her worldly goods along with her—gives me a vivid image of what many adults do when they are caught in the money trap. For Judy, generosity came with maturity. I wish I could say the same is true for everyone! We all need to realize that generosity is God's antidote to greed. If we suspect we are addicted to money or to the possession of what it can buy, we need to develop the habit of regularly giving some of those riches away. Ask yourself if you have developed a real attachment to some possession or other. Look around to see if someone needs that particular thing more than you do. Pray about it. If you are honest, you may realize that the thing has you in its power. Give it away speedily!

A story is told about the queen of the Netherlands who always encouraged her children to give one of their toys to a poor family every Christmas. At first the children would choose toys they did not particularly like or that were broken and needed mending. But the queen would involve herself in the selection process until she was happy they had chosen a favorite toy, one they loved and probably could not replace.

In *Celebration of Discipline,* Richard Foster suggests another healthy exercise: giving as Christmas presents valuable things we already have, instead of buying people new things. God is a great model of that. He did not "buy" the human race a present for Christmas; he gave us the most precious thing he possessed—his one and only Son—a gift he certainly could not replace! Someone has written, "God walked down the stairway of heaven with a baby in his arms." Now *that* is generosity!

Although Jesus himself came to earth as a poor man, he made countless people rich beyond measure. So, too, says Paul, is it with all believers—"having nothing, and yet possessing everything" (2 Cor. 6:10). An unknown author sums up that thought:

> He borrowed a bed to lay his head
> When Christ the Lord came down.
> He borrowed an ass in the mountain pass
> On which to ride to town.
> But the crown that he wore and the cross
>   that he bore
> Were his own—the cross was His own!
> He borrowed a room on the way to his tomb,
> The Passover lamb to eat.
> He borrowed a cave—for him a grave—
> He borrowed a winding sheet.
> But the crown that he wore and the cross
> that he bore
> Were his own—the cross was his own!
> The thorns on his head were worn in my
> stead;

For me the Savior died.
For the guilt of my sin, those nails drove in,
When him they crucified.
Though the crown that He wore
   And the cross that He bore
Were his own—they were justly mine.

Jesus was tempted by the same devil who tempts us. Satan offered the Savior the whole world if he would only worship him. But Jesus was able to keep his focus on the Father, worship him only and not his gifts. We need to focus on the Father as Jesus did. All of us can fall into the trap of being more interested in the perks than the person. Years ago, when Stuart was on the road for weeks on end, the children and I would look forward to our reunion with him with great expectations. We would all go to the airport to meet him. That in itself was a treat. Then we would visit a zoo, a park for a picnic, or a fairground on the way home. We usually had spent lots of time arguing and talking about which of these fun things we would do together to celebrate Daddy's return. When the great day arrived, I would pile the kids into the car and drive the long distance to Manchester airport. Sometimes we would have to wait for a delayed flight or an extra long line in customs. Although the children would have plenty to do, watching everything and everyone, they could hardly wait for Daddy to appear. If we were so thoroughly excited waiting for Stuart to come around the corner, you can imagine my husband's feelings. We at least had had each other. He had been all alone without any of us!

    Suddenly there would be a shout: "Hi, kids. I'm

here!" And three little figures would hurl themselves in Stuart's direction. After a few moments of
excited greetings—a wrestling match with the boys,
a hug for Judy, a big welcome kiss from me—the
kids would cry in unison, "What did you bring us?"

My husband would answer with a grin, "Aren't
you glad to have me back?"

"Yes, yes," the children would answer impatiently,
"but what did you bring us?" Typical, you may say,
and I guess it is. Children are like that. At that stage
in life they were more interested in their father's
gifts than in his presence. Of course, as the children
grew up, their perspective changed. When we get
together as a family now, there is never a thought
of *What did you bring us, Dad?* but rather *Oh, Dad,
how super you are here. We love you!*

So it is, too, when we grow up as Christians. We
learn to worship our Father for his sake alone, and
not for what gifts or blessings he might bring us.
Yet, if we are really honest, we would admit to the
many times we come to him in prayer wondering
what he has for us or asking for something, instead
of wondering what we can give him!

It would be wonderful if we could stop accumu-
lating so much "stuff" and start putting some of it
to eternal use. The secret is keeping our worldly
goods in spiritual perspective and maintaining a
healthy balance. Agur, a wise Old Testament oracle,
prayed: "Give me neither poverty nor riches, but
give me only my daily bread. Otherwise, I may have
too much and disown you and say, 'Who is the
Lord?' Or I may become poor and steal, and so
dishonor the name of my God" (Prov. 30:8-9). The
truly hard thing is to de-accumulate once you have

accumulated! But if we do this, our lives will be a lot less complicated. As Richard Foster says, "Most of us could get rid of half our possessions without any serious sacrifice!"

One way to develop a generosity of spirit is to get involved with missions. Commit to a short-term mission project, contribute to a relief agency, or get involved in a refugee resettlement program in your own city. Also, you could take a family vacation that involves service rather than just pleasure. You and your children would all be all the richer for it.

We tried to give our growing children exposure to others' needs in their own backyards in the good old USA. When David, our eldest, was fifteen, he went on a six-week assignment with about a dozen of his peers and their youth leader to New Orleans. There they lived in a school dormitory and were "servants" to a mission working deep in the French Quarter. It was hard work and quite a culture shock for those kids as they went along on visitations with the staff of the mission, were exposed to life in run-down tenements, and ran children's clubs for the street kids. The young people learned what the other half of the world looks like and lives like, and the experience was life-changing. They were not paid for their work; in fact, it cost them money to go! But they came back with spiritual gold in their spiritual pockets, and that is what mattered. The time spent there was a significant factor in our son's mission-mindedness and in his career choice.

As our children graduated from high school, my husband arranged to take each one with him on a world missions tour. It was designed partly so they could know why he had had to be away from them so much of the time in their growing years. "Across the tracks" in the Third and Fourth World our children saw poverty, disease, and hopelessness first-hand. They met with missionaries serving God in hardship posts where people lived without God, without Christ, and without hope. They watched missionary professionals who could have been making a fortune back home laying up treasure in heaven. None of our children has ever been the same after this experience. It is no surprise to us that they are all in ministry today. If we spend a lot of time building up real wealth—spiritual riches—with our families instead of storing up things for ourselves, chances are that we will become "rich toward God" (Luke 12:21).

These days messages bombard us from every direction, urging us to value the wealthy and those who are visibly important in our society. We must not fall into the trap of thinking that a person's worth can truly be measured in terms of money or power. James says, "Let the believer who is lowly boast in being raised up" (as a believer), because such a person's perspective will possibly be more realistic; the rich believer should remember that though riches may earn him or her a high place as this world sees it, such a person "will disappear like a flower in the field" (1:10, NRSV). After all, James is saying, real status has nothing to do with whether we have a high or low position on earth, but rather with who we are in our relation to God. As Solomon reminded us, "Wealth is worthless in the day of wrath" (Prov. 11:4). Now *that* is the bottom line! None of us will be able to buy God off when we finally stand in front of him in judgment.

Neither will we be able to impress him with our worldly accomplishments, degrees, or titles. The most valuable thing each of us has is the one life we live on earth.

As a Christian author, I am learning not to fall into the money trap. People are kind enough to buy my books after the publisher has been kind enough to publish them. This gives me a modest amount of visibility and status and some cash rewards, but I have to stay very near the Lord about it. I am very well aware that God is not impressed even if some people are! When I get to heaven and ask him "Did you read my book?" he's going to say, "No, but did you read mine?" The more I keep reading his book, the better able I will be to write mine and to keep any earthly rewards in perspective. His Word is all of him. It gives me the inspiration and ideas and ability to acquire wealth. God expects me to keep it all in perspective and invest any profit back into his work, one way or another. Above all, he warns me about the greed-need. I must spend my life for him and not squander it on the world, the flesh, or the devil's bait.

Let us revisit the story of the prodigal son for a moment. After the young man came to his senses and realized that he was in trouble as a result of his own very unwise and ungodly choices, he thought about how well his father's servants were doing. Any one of those men or women was living in better circumstances than he was. He had been a fool to leave it all. Health and wealth and happiness lay in serving his father.

The same is true for us! If there is one way to lay up treasure in heaven, it is by serving our heavenly Father while we are on earth. What happened to the prodigal when he returned home? After the son had put things right with his father and had enjoyed a wonderful homecoming party, his father put him to work. He gave him sandals and a ring. Only sons, not servants, wore sandals, and so when the father told his servants to bring sandals and put them on the boy's bare feet, he was saying in effect, "These sandals are a status symbol. You will serve me as a privileged son, not as a slave." For us, salvation's shoes are a heavenly status symbol, signifying that we are called to serve God the Father as his privileged children.

When the father in the parable put a ring on his son's hand, it was a ring with the father's seal of authority engraved on its face. It carried his signature and the authority to do the father's business in the father's name and for his sake. As the son was sent out to do such transactions, he would be building up the father's estate and bringing honor to him. So, too, as we do the Father's business by going about our daily work, we will be spending the time and money he has given us to extend his kingdom—not our own. And as we bring attention to his name we will find an authority invested in us that will make people sit up and take notice!

The prodigal had walked into the money trap with his eyes wide open. Only after he had spent it all and was bankrupt did he come to himself. I pray we will learn to reject the seduction of greed and so be able to be good stewards of whatever goods and currency are given to us by the Lord. I pray he will say to us at the end of each day, "Well done, good and faithful servant!" (Matt. 25:21).

Know, however, that if we succumb and find ourselves over our heads in money troubles, God is strong enough to lift up the spring of the trap and set us free. Let us each try to "guard [our] heart, for it is the wellspring of life" (Prov. 4:23). It is the love of money, not money itself, that is the root of all kinds of evil (1 Tim. 6:10). If we love the Lord with all our heart, soul, mind, and strength, we will be all right. And if we truly love our neighbor as ourselves, we will find plenty of places to invest the little or much that God has entrusted us with. One way or another, we all will have to give an accounting of our stewardship to our Master who is the Chief Steward. That alone ought to be enough to keep us clear of the money trap!

Over twenty years ago, God tested me on this very thing. We had been living and working for Christ in Great Britain for a number of years, but had just accepted a call to a pastorate in the USA. The church that called us suggested we sell almost everything and come with only our clothes and a few precious personal items. At first it appeared to be an easy assignment to fulfill. After all, I thought, we had been living on a very low salary and trying to maintain a very simple lifestyle, so selling most of our belongings should not have made any difference. Yet, as I got into practicalities and the realities of the exercise, I found myself surprisingly reluctant. God had to take my clutching fingers and pry them off the "things" I had been so sure were not possessing my heart. "Hold them lightly, not tightly," he gently reminded me. It was a good lesson and one I try to revisit when I find myself facing the money trap today. Scott Wesley Brown says it wonderfully in his song:

Things

Things upon the mantle, things on every shelf
things that others gave me, things I gave myself.
Things I've stored in boxes, that don't mean much
  anymore,
old magazines and memories, behind the attic door.

Things on hooks and hangers, things on ropes and
  rings,
things I guard that blind me to the pettiness of
  things.
Am I like the rich young ruler, ruled by all I own?
If Jesus came and asked me, could I leave them all
  alone?

Oh, Lord, I look to heaven, beyond the veil of time
to gain eternal insight that nothing's really mine—
And to only ask for daily bread and all content-
  ment brings,
to find freedom as Your servant—in the midst of
  all these things.

For discarded in the junk yards, and rusting in the
  rain,
lie things that took the finest years of lifetimes to
  obtain.
And whistling through these tombstones the
  hollow breezes sing
a song of dreams surrendered to the tyranny of
  things.

We must never surrender our dreams to "the tyranny of things." We must stay close to Jesus and
dream his dreams, reach for his star, and live only
and always in the here and now with the bright
light of eternity before us. Years ago, I came across
an anonymous poem that has served me well when
I am tantalized by greed:

To Gather Wealth or Gather Grace

When the great plants of our cities have turned
    out their last finished work,
When the merchants have sold their last yard of
    silk and dismissed their last tired clerk,
When the banks have raked in their last shilling
    and paid to dividend,
And the Judge of the earth says, "Close for the
    night," and asks for a balance . . .
What Then?

When the actor has played his last drama and the
    mimic has made his last fun,
When the movie has flashed its last picture and the
    billboard displayed its last run,
When the crowds seeking pleasure have vanished
    and gone into the darkness again,
And the world that's rejected its Savior is asked for
    an answer . . .
What Then?

When the bugle's call sinks into silence and the
    long marching columns stand still,
When the captain has given his last orders and
    they've captured the last fort and hill,
When the flag has been hauled from the masthead
    and the wounded afield checked in,
And the trumpet of ages is sounded and you stand
    before him . . .
What Then?

When the people have heard their last sermon and
    the preacher has prayed his last prayer,
When the choir has sung its last anthem and the
    sound has died out on the air,
When the Bible lies closed on the altar and the
    pews are all empty of men,
And each one stands facing his record and the
    great book is opened . . .
What Then?

When life, friend, has run to a finish, when the last
thing you can do is done,
When your life here on earth is ended and
eternity's issues begun,
As you think of how long God has pleaded, of
how Christ bore your sins on the tree,
And your soul stands there naked before him and
the Father denies you . . .
What Then?

If we could only live in the light of the *What then?*
the *What now?* would take good care of itself. This
is what we must return to over and over again as
we choose to view money God's way throughout
our lives.

Study Guide: The Money Trap
For Personal Growth and/or Group Discussion

1. Read James 1:9-11; James 5:1-6; and 1 Timothy 6:17-19. What concept or illustration or teaching about money and possessions struck you from these verses or from this chapter?
   5 minutes

2. Read Exodus 20:17 (the tenth commandment). The word covet means wanting what other people have. The darker side of coveting is wanting those people *not* to have what they have! Such an attitude can lead to all sorts of evil and mischief. Make a list of all the things mentioned in this verse that we should not covet, and then identify their modern counterparts.   *15 minutes*

1.	1.
2.	2.
3.	3.
4.	4.
5.	5.
6.	6.
7.	7.

   Circle the thing that is most tempting for you to covet.

3. Read Christ's injunction in Luke 12:33. How does this apply to the modern-day Christian?
   10 minutes

4. Choose one of these warning examples from Scripture to discuss and think about. (Read verses before and after the listed reference to get an idea of the context.) *10 minutes*
   (a) Achan: Joshua 7:21
   (b) Judas: Matthew 26:15
   (c) Felix: Acts 24:26

Prayer Time   *10 minutes*

1. Praise God for his many benefits. "Count your many blessings, name them one by one."

2. Pray for those who are rich that they will use their resources for God's kingdom. Pray for yourself in this regard.

3. Pray for those who live in the poverty of affluence without Christ.

3

To Speak Wisely or Foolishly

The Mouth Trap

Someone has said, "A Christian is a mind through which Christ thinks, a heart through which Christ loves, and a voice through which Christ speaks." There is so much we can do with our tongues for good or for evil. Jesus said "Whatever is in your heart determines what you say. A good person produces good words from a good heart, and an evil person produces evil words from an evil heart" (Matt. 12:34-35, NLT). What is *in* must come *out*. If the Holy Spirit is going to use our mouths to his advantage, we must choose to make sure that what is in our hearts is worth listening to.

Of course, it goes without saying—but I will say

it anyway—that our lives must speak louder than our words. As we seek to pass our faith onto others, we need to remember Francis of Assisi's words: "Preach the gospel all the time. If necessary use words!" There is one group of people, however, with a need to be particularly careful not to have a double standard where actions and words are concerned. Those of us who have the gift and opportunity of being public speakers on the Lord's behalf will be watched very carefully and held strictly accountable for our words.

James reminds us that teachers of God's Word have a great privilege and also a great responsibility. The position of a religious leader should not be taken lightly or coveted for reasons of pride or self-aggrandizement. The pulpit, as John R. W. Stott has most aptly said, "is a dangerous place for any son of Adam." Or, I would add, "any daughter of Eve." James points out that a teacher, in fact, will be "judged with greater strictness" by God, adding that "all of us make many mistakes. Anyone who makes no mistakes in speaking is perfect, able to keep the whole body in check with a bridle." (3:1-2, NRSV).

James is saying that all of us are vulnerable to the sin of pride, and no one is to think he or she has "arrived" spiritually. This is a charge to be humble. James constantly warns us against arrogance. Humility links us to God, whereas pride disrupts our relationship with him. If we are out of touch with the power the Lord offers us to live a holy and good life, we will be out of control. James tells us, however, that as we are connected to God, we will be able to control what we say and what we do! "Humility that comes from wisdom" (3:13) strengthens that connection.

James makes his point with several illustrations. The first has to do with horses, bits, and bridles; the second, with boats. Both images have to do with steering and so refer to the path of one's life. James writes, "When we put bits into the mouths of horses to make them obey us, we can turn the whole animal. Or take ships as an example. Although they are so large and are driven by strong winds, they are steered by a very small rudder. . . . Likewise the tongue is a small part of the body, but it makes great boasts" (3:3-5). James then changes the picture and asks us to "consider what a great forest is set on fire by a small spark. The tongue also is a fire, a world of evil among the parts of the body. It corrupts the whole person, sets the whole course of his life on fire, and is itself set on fire by hell" (3:5-6).

One reason I enjoy James's letter so much is that he loved to use imagery. I, too, like to use pictures when I write and speak. Somehow it helps people remember important points. Fire is an especially vivid image. Fire spreads, and I have no doubt James picked this analogy because of the incredibly rapid-spreading firepower of words. James was concerned about individuals who have no control of their tongues and use them to speak evil. He knew that what we say will not only affect others but will also affect us! Evil words will spread like fire to all areas of our own life, causing us to burn with rage against other people. We may be so consumed with anger that we might even be driven to violence against them. James depicts the tongue's wickedness as a conflagration spreading through the time span of a person's life as well as through the complex diversity of one's behavior. The true origin of the tongue's blazing power to destroy is Satan and hell—It "is itself set on fire by hell" (3:6).

We have all experienced this in some measure. Maybe we have immolated someone's reputation with our words, or have been the victim of such destructive influences ourselves. Sometimes an uncomplimentary remark about someone just pops out of my mouth. And before I know it, I am horrified to find those words burning into my thinking and spreading throughout my personality. And the fire may instigate action by other parts of my body. My hands may pick up a pen and paper to express my hot words to the person in question, and my feet may then take the letter to the mailbox! Once a fire really gets going, it is almost impossible to stop it.

Picking up a different analogy, James comments, "Every species of beast and bird, of reptile and sea creature, can be tamed and has been tamed by the human species, but no one can tame the tongue"(3:7-8, NRSV). The wild animal out of its cage presents another negative picture of what the tongue can do. It can rip its victim to shreds. It can tear a relationship to bits. Sometimes, as my husband and I sit in a marriage-counseling session, I am awestruck by the force and the truth of what James is saying about the devastation the untamed tongue can cause. His last image says it all: "It is a restless evil, full of deadly poison" (v. 8). Satan-the-snake bites!

Of course, Satan must find it easy to control the tongue of the unbeliever. But James is talking to Christians in these words. Is he therefore just trying for a dramatic effect? I think not. Anyone who has been involved in a knock-down, drag-out fight in a church can testify to the prevalence of "snakebite" in a congregational meeting. Believers can fall into the mouth trap, eat the poisoned cheese Satan has set there, and become the very voice of hell itself! And that is scary. We have a record of Jesus pointing out the dangers of the tongue, too. After Jesus predicted his own death, Peter tried to persuade him not to go up to Jerusalem, where his suffering was to occur. In Peter's words, Jesus heard the voice of Satan trying to divert him from the Cross. The Lord said to Peter, "Get behind me, Satan! You are a stumbling block to me; for you are setting your mind not on divine things but on human things" (Matt. 16:23, NRSV).

Because we must constantly be aware of the possibility of our tongues being a "restless evil, full of deadly poison," James points out the incongruity of talking out of both sides of our mouth:

> With [the tongue] we bless the Lord and Father, and with it we curse those who are made in the likeness of God. From the same mouth come blessing and cursing. My brothers and sisters, this ought not to be so. Does a spring pour forth from the same opening both fresh and brackish water? Can a fig tree, my brothers and sisters, yield olives, or a grapevine figs? No more can salt water yield fresh (3:9-12, NRSV).

I think all of us at some time or other have wished we could cut out our untamed tongue! A friend shared one of those moments with me. She belonged to a small church in England way out in the country. The parishioners had problems attracting visitors. They would try this and that, but nothing seemed to work. Then one day to their delight, some visitors came. There were just three of them, two women and a small child. The fellowship my friend belonged to did not have a minister of its own as it was not large enough to support a preacher, so they had "pulpit supply" each week. This particular day, the preacher was awful! My friend felt excited about the newcomers but watched them looking around and fidgeting. She said to herself, "Why did they have to come this week?" As soon as the service was over, she rushed up to them and said, "I'm so glad you're here. We just love having visitors, but I just want to apologize for the guest speaker. They're not usually quite so boring!" One of the women smiled a tight smile and replied, "That's my husband, and this is his sister." My friend's mouth dropped open, and she mumbled, "Oh, dear, I'm so sorry." And the lady said bitingly, "I'm not!" And that was that.

Many of us have had a problem with "foot and mouth disease" to a lesser or greater degree. James tells us that genuine religion should and must affect the tongue. Proverbs says, "A wise man holds his tongue, only a fool blurts out everything he knows. That only leads to sorrow and trouble" (Prov. 21:23, author's translation). James adds, "Anyone who makes no mistakes in speaking is perfect" (3:2, NRSV). What does that mean? Who can be perfect? The word *perfect* in this context means mature at the stage where you are—able to keep your "whole body in check."

We have just enjoyed a visit with two of our six grandchildren. As a proud grandma, I think the six-year-old is a perfect six-year-old, and the four-year-old a perfect four-year-old. They are "perfect" for the stage where they are. Being a Christian means that our speech will reflect our spiritual maturity. Even a six-year-old can control his tongue. You might not think so, but in my experience a six-year-old who is told not to say a naughty word has the ability to avoid saying it.

Paul, writing to the Corinthians, said, "When I was a child, I talked like a child, I thought like a child. . . . When I became a man, I put childish ways behind me" (1 Cor. 13:11). He was saying in essence, "One day I grew up." Unfortunately, there is a childishness about some Christians. They are still talking like little kids. They may have been Christians for years and years, but they have never grown up spiritually. You can tell that because they cannot control their tongues.

Well, then, thinking of this analogy, how do children speak? For one thing, they tattle. A child will come and tell you what the others are doing, especially if they should not be doing it. Our small son David would often come to me and say, "You should just see what Judy's doing, Mummy!" When kids tell tales, they are really hoping they get their siblings into trouble. You have to deal with that. So you say things like, "I don't want to hear what Judy's doing, David. Off you go and play." And David goes and plays, and then you go and see what Judy's doing. But you do not let him know that!

Kids are not averse to telling untruths as well. Remember, we were all born with a sinful nature. My dear mom used to get really upset with me when I suggested that her darling grandchildren had been born with a sinful nature. Because she was not a believer at the time, she felt that all kids were perfect until we messed them up. My mother believed in the inherent goodness of human nature, so it was really hard to convince her that however perfect she thought her grandchildren were, they had in fact been born with sinful little hearts. "I never taught them how to answer back or tell lies, Mother," I pointed out. "Who crept into my house and taught them how to do these things? They just know how to do them all on their own!"

We have in us an innate propensity to use our tongues to speak evil because we are evil at heart. Even though Christ has through grace brought his nature into our lives, our old sinful nature gets out of control sometimes and predominates. Therefore, we need to ration our words. Proverbs 10:19 tells us wisely, "Don't talk so much. You keep putting your foot in your mouth. Be sensible and turn off the flow!" (TLB). What was it James said? A salt spring cannot produce fresh water. Bitter water needs staunching or it will taint all that it touches. We need to turn off the flow of bitterness.

The tongue is so small a member, yet so large in its potential for trouble. James has used pictures of a boat turned at will by a tiny rudder or a horse made to obey by bit and bridle. The idea is that God wants to control us, to pull us in. A bit or rudder turns the horse or ship exactly where the rider or captain wants it to go, so everything depends on who is riding the horse or steering the vessel! If our old selfish nature is in the saddle or at the helm, it will turn our conversation in any old direction that it wants. I like to think of the Gospel account of Palm Sunday, with Jesus riding his little donkey, a wild animal that had never been entirely broken in. But Jesus took the reins in his hands and turned the little animal wherever he wanted it to go. That is how our tongues can be controlled. We can ask Jesus to "ride" our old nature and help us. We can give him permission to bridle our tongue.

Think about how Jesus wonderfully bridled his own tongue. Think of all the times it must have been hard for him to keep quiet. The last time he saw the disciples in the upper room, for example, he said to them, "I have much more to say to you, more than you can now bear" (John 16:12). He told them that when the Holy Spirit came, he would explain things further. Can you imagine if you or I had knowledge that today was the last time we would be with those closest to us? Our first inclination would be to talk our heads off, whether or not those listening were able to understand us. Jesus, out of love and concern for his disciples, knew there was "a time to be silent and a time to speak" (Eccles. 3:7), and that this was a time to keep silent. And so he did. His Spirit, which he sent to live in us, can help us to do the same!

All through Jesus' ministry, people wondered at the gracious words that came out of his mouth. No bitter water sprang from the lips of the Lord Jesus! Maybe strong words, maybe fierce words or righteously angry words, but above all, they were gracious words. So Jesus in me can help me bridle my tongue, control my temper, and choose fitting words for me to speak that meet any and all situations. When our tongue starts to lead us into rough waters, we have got to allow the Pilot to turn our ship about and steer us to safety.

How does this work? Imagine chatting to a group of women in the church foyer. Somebody says, "Did you know that Mrs. Adam has been appointed head of the Christian education department?" So far so good. There we are, sailing along like a little ship on Lake Placid. The tongue, however, can steer the conversation any way it wants it to go. It can say, for instance, "It's such a pity that her kids are in trouble." Suddenly Lake Placid has turned into a whirlpool—and Mrs. Adam is in big trouble. On the other hand, we could say, "Mrs. Adam is a great choice. She can really identify with all of us who have had some bad moments with our kids. She's learning so much by seeing her own children right in the middle of all that peer pressure just now. She'll be able to help us all a great deal."

If we do not want our words to cause someone a shipwreck, we need to give Jesus the rudder. Have you ever done that? You can kneel down and say, "Jesus, it says in the Bible that all my members must be yielded to you. My hands, my feet, my heart, my mind, my ears, my eyes, and *my tongue.*" If you think about each of the parts of your body, especially the tongue, and give them one by one to God and ask him to control them, he will.

God takes seriously the words of all his followers: not just teachers, but listeners and learners, too. Jesus said, "I tell you this, that you must give an account on judgment day of every idle word you speak" (Matt. 12:36, NLT). Paul told the Christians in Colosse, "Be wise in the way you act toward outsiders; make the most of every opportunity. Let your conversation be always full of grace, seasoned with salt, so that you may know how to answer everyone" (Col. 4:56). Let your speech always be gracious, he said. Not *sometimes* gracious, not just gracious in the church lobby on Sunday, but *always* gracious.

Although James used *salt* to connote impurity, Paul gives the word a positive meaning. In Jesus' day, when the fishermen brought in their catch of fish, they would put them in big baskets. Then they would take great blocks of salt, crush them up with a stone, and spread the salt all over the fish. Without refrigeration in such a hot climate, fishermen required the salt to arrest decay and corruption in their catch. Keep that picture in your head, and every time you are talking your head off, shut your eyes quickly and "season" your words with salt. That means you will temper unkind criticism with a kind word about the person, tell a gossip you would rather not hear the latest red-hot news, or quietly seek to be a peacemaker between two people having an argument.

Salting a conversation also includes telling someone that certain expressions offend you. There are words that are obviously off limits for the believer. We call such talk profanity. "With [the tongue] we bless the Lord and Father, and with it we curse those who are made in the likeness of God" says James (3:9, NRSV). Now cursing, or impure language, takes many forms. One of the forms is obscenity. That is something we must not do! It is one of our Father God's no-nos for his children. Having just spent time with my small grandchildren, it seems like I did not say yes, yes once. It was all no, no. I wish I could have said yes, yes more often. But when you are looking after three toddlers, what can you do?

Blasphemy, of course, is one of God's no-nos. As

the ten commandments have it "Thou shalt not take the name of the Lord thy God in vain" (Exod. 20:7, KJV). This commandment should be like a bridle on our tongue. The Lord will not hold guiltless anyone who misuses his name. He will look on such persons as criminals and will severely punish them. In Old Testament times people would be stoned to death for using the name of the Lord irreverently. This is a serious matter, and God has not changed his mind about his rules!

That kind of profanity includes speaking frivolously of God. When I first met my husband and was a very new convert, I loved to talk about Jesus. My speech would be peppered with "Jesus this, Jesus that, Jesus the other." One day Stuart asked me, "Why don't you say 'the Lord Jesus'?" I asked why I needed to do that, and he said, "When you say 'Jesus this' or 'Jesus that,' it sounds irreverent—almost too familiar. It jars." I thought about that and decided if I was going to really treat Jesus' name with the esteem it deserved, I was not going to use it that way anymore. And now when I talk about the Lord, I try to refer to him as "the Lord Jesus"; somehow that sounds so much better. This attitude affects my writing habits, too. When I began writing (and I write longhand), I could never bring myself to write *JC* to refer to the Lord. Avoiding that abbreviation is one little way I help myself to think reverently. We have to start with little things—if we treat the name of the Lord as it should be treated in the little things, we will start to do so in the big things as well.

Have you noticed people around you at a ball game or in a public place using the Lord's name "in vain"? It hurts. Stuart and I were once sitting at the airport on our way to Denver, and there was a man in a very nice business suit sitting behind us with three or four of his colleagues. We were all waiting for the same plane. The men looked like high-class people, but when they opened their mouths their language was unbelievable. I kept looking at Stuart and thinking, *I don't know if I can take this much longer.* I was just about to turn around and say, "Hey, that's my Friend and Lord you're talking about!" when the call came for the plane and I did not get the opportunity. If such irreverence gets to us, can you imagine how it makes God feel when people swear on his name or even speak lightly of him?

People who speak lightly of the Lord are indicating that they take their faith lightly, too. "God's name is blasphemed among the Gentiles because of you," says Paul (Rom. 2:24). Paul was talking to Jewish people who professed to be teachers of the law of God but were living as if they were infidels. Their lives were speaking volumes about their double-mindedness. Addressing such a teacher as one who considered himself "an instructor of the foolish, a teacher of infants," Paul challenged, "You, then, who teach others, do you not teach yourself? You who preach against stealing, do you steal? You who say that people should not commit adultery, do you commit adultery? You who abhor idols, do you rob temples? You who brag about the law, do you dishonor God by breaking the law? As it is written: 'God's name is blasphemed among the Gentiles because of you'" (Rom. 2:20-24).

And now we see James bringing the same warning to Christian believers. He could well have used Paul's words: "You, then, who teach others, do you not teach yourself?" James tells all of us, "Do not merely listen to the word, and so deceive yourselves. Do what it says" (1:22). Especially when it comes to the tongue!

James's words have come home to me on many different occasions. When I first began to travel and speak, I used to have to get where I was going by plane. Before coming to the United States in 1970, I had flown very little. I did not like it! In fact, I would be extremely nervous whenever I got onto a plane. I would hope the seats were evenly balanced and would worry about the weather. Every little bump would turn my stomach upside down, so I would try to distract myself by getting out my speech and reviewing it, and usually I was planning to speak on "faith" or "peace of mind" or some such subject. In the back of my mind, I would hear Paul's words—"You who teach others, do you not teach yourself?" No, I was not committing adultery, worshiping idols, stealing, or any other such no-no, but I could not in all good conscience get off that plane and talk about faith or peace of mind! I realized that I needed God's help in overcoming my unreasonable fear of flying before my tongue could teach others much, certainly concerning the subject of faith. The people listening would not have thought much of me or my God if I continued being such a hypocrite. God has wonderfully overcome these very real fears as I have applied my own teaching to myself and put into practice some biblical principles of trust and dependence.

Here is our big problem: When we do not practice what we preach, we discredit not only ourselves, but the One we preach about. In other words, a scraggly, ill-kempt sheep can reflect a distorted image of the Good Shepherd.

One day during a trip to Israel, I was standing in Jerusalem watching some sheep come down the road into the city. I looked both ways and saw there were two flocks coming toward the market gate from different directions. One was coming from the right and another from the left. The ones on the right were fat, fluffy things. They were so cute—trotting along happily one behind the other and almost holding on to each other's tails. They looked well fed, and I could imagine smiles on their little sheep faces. Their shepherd walked proudly in front, leading them along. From the other direction came the other flock, and what a difference I saw! These sheep were scrawny and dirty. One of them had an ear hanging by a shred. Their shepherd was not really watching them, and they were wandering all over the place. I thought to myself, *If I were a sheep, I know which flock I'd rather belong to!* I found myself judging the shepherds by the way their sheep looked and behaved. That is what people do in the spiritual realm, too. They judge the Shepherd by his sheep.

"Well, Jill," you might say, "fear of flying, or lack of control of my tongue, or profanity isn't really my problem. I hardly ever fly and I never swear." But what about mere idle words? In the Scriptures, *idle words* refers to remarks we do not even think about. How many times a week do you say, "Oh, God" or "Oh, Christ"? Perhaps such words had been so much a part of your language before you found Jesus that you have brought them right along with you. I had a problem with these words before I became a Christian. I did not think I did; I was just totally immersed in my culture. Yet, after I became a Christian, when I would open my mouth to use my familiar "idle words," it was just as if somebody tapped me on the shoulder and said, "Don't do that anymore." The Holy Spirit was checking me. You can ask the Holy Spirit to alert you, too. You can pray, *Holy Spirit, if you see me unthinkingly about to use an expression that is a derivation of your name, stop me.* He will be delighted to answer that prayer.

Golly, gosh, and *oh, heavens* are idle words, too. Jesus warns us, "Do not swear at all: either by heaven, for it is God's throne; or by the earth, for it is his footstool. . . . Simply let your 'Yes' be 'Yes,' and your 'No,' 'No'; anything beyond this comes from the evil one" (Matt. 5:34-37).

If you have children, they need to know about all this at an early age. I remember when Peter, our youngest child, started school and came home with a whole barrel full of bad words. One night I said to him, "Peter, you have been coming home saying all sorts of new words. Do you know what these new words you're learning mean? They're very naughty words. They're bad words."

He said, "Which words, Mummy?"

I replied, "Pete, you know which words."

"No, Mummy, I don't," he said innocently. "If you'll tell me, then I'll know."

Well, I was pretty sure he knew, but what could I do? So I said to him, "Pete, I will say them once so you will know from now on which words you are never to say. But you'll only hear Mummy say them this one time."

"All right, Mummy," he answered with a grin.

So I went through my list. After each word, Pete cringed and pulled faces (he's a real actor). When we got to the end of the list, the little rascal said, "You forgot two words, Mummy!" So he knew perfectly well all the time. He just wanted to make me say them. Well, it turned out to be an excellent thing to do. The policy had been specifically stated, and now I could call him on it. Perhaps we all need to spell out the "bad language" rules for our kids so they know exactly what we mean.

Since we have all been made in God's image, cursing another human being is like cursing God. "Damn you!" is a curse, as is "Go to hell!" Cursing, though, is a little different from obscenity or irreverence. It is something we are going to be held accountable for. A curse is an angry, abusive word to someone we consider our subordinate. It can also be a bitter denunciation in that person's absence. That kind of talk is all part of the "filthy language" that Paul says is a no-no (Col. 3:8).

Now let us move on to something of which most of us are guilty—nagging. Nagging is all sorts of things, but it, too, comes from an untamed tongue—an unbroken horse, a ship out of control. One of the best illustrations of nagging is in the book of Job. Job had had a terrible day. (It had to be a Monday!) If you read chapter 1, you can see what happened to him. He lost his house, his business, and all his kids. His land, cattle, sheep, and servants were all gone as well. In fact, he lost everything but his wife! Poor Job. When the devil put his finger on all those other things, he must have thought, *What's the worst thing I could do to Job? I know—I'll leave him his wife!* That's the sort of woman she was.

Years ago, I wrote a book called *Prime Rib and Apple*. It was about all the "prime ribs" of the Bible, starting with Eve. When I came to Job's wife, I called her "little dripping tap." Perhaps in America we should call her "little dripping faucet." To me, Job's wife was like a dripping faucet; she just dripped, dripped, dripped all day long, making Job's misery worse.

Job's wife, you see, was a nagger. She suggested that Job should curse God and commit suicide. What an empathetic, supportive helpmate! Job told her she was talking like a foolish, evil woman. As the bitter water flowed out of her heart, she was talking like an unbeliever. All of us can do that, and nagging is one way we do it. Nag, nag, nag. Nagging is reminding somebody about something over and over again. Nagging could be defined as "unforgiveness showing," because when people go on and on and on about something, it is often because they are harboring a grudge. If you point it out to them, they may well say, "Oh, yes, I have forgiven that person." But if they are nagging, chances are that they have not, and they are showing their lack of forgiveness by bringing up the matter over and over again.

I could not help overhearing a conversation on an airplane the other day. A husband and wife were talking. "Are you going to forget my birthday again like you did last year?" asked the wife. That is nagging! That is unforgiveness showing. So is the mother's comment to her teenager: "Don't be late this time like you were last time, and the time before that, and the time before that!" The book of Proverbs says, "Better to live on a corner of the roof than share a house with a quarrelsome wife" (Prov.

25:24). If you are married and realize you are a nagger, ask your husband to help you turn off the dripping faucet. Often, just being honest about the hidden resentment and disappointment behind your nagging will improve the situation on the other person's part, reducing whatever triggers your nagging. (If you are not married, ask a friend for help.) Ann Landers says, "Nagging is like being nibbled to death by a duck." I really do not know exactly what she meant, but it is very descriptive. She captures the unpleasantness of the experience quite well.

And then there is *gossip*—the needless repetition of someone's real or imaginary faults or intimate details of his or her life. "The tongue is a small part of the body, but it makes great boasts. Consider what a great forest is set on fire by a small spark," warns James (3:5). Remember the great Chicago fire? What got that going? Well, some say a cow kicked over a lamp and sent sparks flying into the hay. It only takes one spark to get a fire going. When I used to go to visit my kids (who were living in Menominee, Michigan), I would travel through a little town that is famous for a fire that was even worse than the Chicago fire. The story is fascinating. The whole town was wiped out because the air caught fire! This was because of a paper factory in the area. The resin in the air ignited, and most of the populace was suffocated. So, too, can we set the very air around us on fire by gossip.

When James says that the tongue can make the whole of life a blazing hell (3:6), the word he actually uses is *Gehenna*. Gehenna was the valley where the people burned all the rubbish from the city of Jerusalem. It made a terrible stink! That is what gossip is like. Somebody says, "Don't carry this any further; it needs to be confidential." But you do carry it further—often to the very next person you meet. "A gossip goes about telling secrets, but one who is trustworthy in spirit keeps a confidence" (Prov. 11:13, NRSV). What we all need to do is to be trustworthy and to say, "I'll find something nice to say or I won't say anything at all." Gossip so often causes the innocent to suffer and the forgiven to wonder if they really have been forgiven.

The tongue is very good at meting out little personal animosities. Because gossip has to do with malice or retaliation, it gets under our skin. In his book *No Wonder They Call Him the Savior* (Multnomah, 1990), Max Lucado writes, "Maybe your wound is old; though the arrow was extracted long ago the arrowhead is still lodged, hidden under your skin." The apostle Peter tells us that "when they hurled their insults at him [the Lord Jesus], he did not retaliate; when he suffered, he made no threats. Instead, he entrusted himself to him who judges justly" (1 Peter 2:23). Jesus did not bite back (or backbite). He never said, "I'll get you for this!" He did not say, "Just wait until after the resurrection, buddy." He entrusted himself to the One who judges justly—to God, his heavenly Father.

Think about the other side of the story for a minute. If you are the victim of a malicious tongue—it is not your tongue that has been causing the trouble—what do you do then? Well, the apostle Paul had been on the receiving end of gossip, insults, and false accusations, but he was able to say to the church in Corinth, "I care very little if I am judged by you or by any human court; indeed, I do not even judge myself. . . . It is the Lord who judges me" (1 Cor. 4:3-4). He does not say that he is innocent of any wrongdoing, but that human judgment is fallible, so he is not going to let people's criticism get to him.

When I am criticized, I find it helps if I consider the source. Sometimes my critics have an axe to grind. Perhaps they are going through something really difficult themselves, and I just happened along at the wrong moment. Paul said, "I don't worry over what you think about this [whether he was a good servant of God]" (1 Cor. 4:3, TLB). It all depends who the *you* is. In Paul's case, he considered the source and realized he was being attacked by jealous and hostile people who were caught firmly in the mouth trap. He also refused to spend too much time in introspection: "I don't even trust my own judgment on this point" (v. 3, TLB). Instead, he committed himself to God, who judges the motives of human hearts. I can safely trust God when I am criticized because he knows why I am being attacked and how I feel about it in *my* heart. He is scrupulously fair. If my conscience is clear, I can safely leave the whole matter with him, knowing he will defend me one day. I do not need to preempt the last judgment! So if I am being judged by a fellow human being, I do not need to judge back. There is only one judgment seat, and it is most thoroughly occupied!

Proverbs has much to say about the tongue. The writer (probably Solomon) tells us there are six things that God hates. Three of the six have to do with the tongue. One of the things God hates is slander. A slanderer finds fault with the demeanor or conduct of others and spreads around innuendos and criticisms about them. According to James, this kind of talk is "full of deadly poison" (3:8). "The poison of vipers," echoes Paul, "is on their lips" (Rom. 3:13). There is always a bit of truth in slander, and that is what makes it so dangerous. It is an exaggeration of faults, a coloring of circumstances. Though perhaps no direct falsehood, by leaving out some details and including others, it is a thorough misrepresentation of a person's motives or actions.

We can understand slander by looking at the image of two painters painting the same still-life group of objects. One painting has the objects in perspective, like a photograph. The other artist looks at the same grouping and blows some items all out of proportion. That is what slander does. You can stop slander by saying something like, "Now, we don't really know all the facts, do we?" Or you can say, "Why don't we find out what really happened?" Or "Let's go and ask the people concerned if this is really how it is." Remember that the devil is often spoken of as "the accuser." We must be careful not to do his work for him.

In the end, our use of the tongue for good or for ill comes down to who we really are inside. An ancient sage once said, "Speak, that I may see thee." You might have expected him to say, "Speak, that I may hear thee." But no—he meant exactly what he said. Who we are expresses itself in the words we speak. As we come to know Christ and he makes us more and more like him, we come to sound as if we really are Christians in our hearts.

If "Out of the overflow of the heart the mouth speaks" (Matt. 12:34), the only course we can follow is to spend much time alone with the Lord Jesus, so that our heart is filled with an abundance of his love and wisdom. A cup filled with sweet water cannot spill one bitter drop, even when jogged. Whenever people heard Jesus Christ speak, they exclaimed, "What gracious words!" May they always say the same of us.

Study Guide: The Mouth Trap
For Personal Growth and/or Group Discussion

1. Read James 3:3-8. Which of the pictures of "the power of the tongue" struck you particularly and why? *6 minutes*

   (a) horses
   (b) ships
   (c) forest fire
   (d) snakebite (venom)

2. Read James 3:9 and Genesis 1:26-27. Cursing a human being is the same as cursing God. How should this affect our speech? *5 minutes*

3. Read Colossians 4:5-6. What does it mean to "season our speech with salt"? Why is it so important? Discuss Matthew 5:34. What do you think it means for us today? *6 minutes*

4. Review and define *profanity*, which has many meanings, putting each of these in your own words. *10 minutes*

   (a) obscenity
   (b) idle words
   (c) cursing
   (d) nagging
   (e) gossip

Prayer Time   *5 minutes*

1. Pray about all you have learned about the mouth trap.

2. Pray for those who use language that they should not use around your children. If the offenders are other children, turn your concern into motivation to lead them to Christ.

3. Pray for church leaders who are subjected to criticism.

   Meditate on this: If you are being criticized by someone already caught in the mouth trap, the answer is not to join them in the trap, but to commit yourself to the true judge, Jesus, and use the opportunity to show a gracious spirit.

4

To Value Our Time or Fritter It Away

The Minute Trap

A few years ago, Stuart and I received an invitation to return to England and conduct some meetings. Ever since we emigrated to the USA in 1970, we had had numerous opportunities to return to our homeland; but this time would be unusual for we would be meeting up with many of the people we had worked with during our twelve years in British evangelism. During the flight over the Atlantic, I tried to recall the names and appearances of the couples with whom we would be sharing the week's ministry. When we eventually arrived at the conference, I got quite a shock. I had been remembering them all as we had left them. To my chagrin, most of the men were bald, and most of the women gray-haired! I had quite forgotten the passage of time. Then I took another look in the mirror and realized anew what the Scottish poet Robert Burns said so well, "Nae man can tether time or tide."

How many times have you heard someone complain, "I never have enough minutes in my day"? Yet we all have as many minutes as everyone else— no more, no less. Time can fly when we are busy or having fun and it can drag when we are bored and lonely. After young lovers said good-bye in war-torn Britain, it seemed an eternity before the soldier-husbands had some leave. But once the longed-for leave arrived and loved ones shared precious moments together, time seemed to run out almost as soon as the reunion began. Time's velocity is actually the same for all of us. It is our choices and expectations and the events we experience that seem to affect its speed.

When we lived in Britain, my husband needed to be away a great deal, often for months at a time. He would visit the other youth centers that were part of our organization and also respond to preaching invitations from around the world. The times he was actually home were brief and packed with work as well. I would find that the time we had with Stuart around the campus just flew by. Even when he was not actually in the house, we were conscious that he was nearby, but I wanted to put the brakes on the rushing moments and screech to a halt. At the end of a period when he was home, we would all pile into the car, take him to the airport, and wave good-bye. The journey back to our house without him—exactly the same distance as the one coming to the airport—always appeared twice as long. "Are we nearly there?" the kids would ask over and over. They had not asked that question once when Daddy was in the car!

The next twelve or so weeks without Dad would pass at different speeds, too. The first four always went pretty slowly. I found ways to help myself, like hanging a twelve-week calendar in the kitchen so one of us could check off the days one by one. But I never even put it up until a month had gone by. Then we would have a great time crossing off a whole four weeks of very long days. When we were in the middle part, with a lump of time behind us, the time seemed to quicken to almost normal pace. Then there were only four weeks left, and all but the last of those would clip along fairly rapidly. The last week was the worst! Talk about time dragging! I had plenty of opportunities to see that what is going on in our lives determines how we experience and spend the moments we have.

For some people, there is never enough time in a day to do all the things they need and want to do. For others, time is just an agonizing reality. They can even get so depressed that they decide they want out of it altogether. We need to realize that God considers time as an extremely important commodity. He knows that eternal destinies are decided during our earthly moments, and in his grace and mercy he gives people plenty of time to come to know and trust him.

Satan, on the other hand, wishes to use time to rob us of eternity. He works overtime, never takes a vacation, and tries to make every moment count. His goal is to seduce us into false confidence: "You have all the time in the world," he tells us. "Take your ease—eat, drink, and be merry." He suggests that the only thing that matters is the here-and-now and seeks to divert us completely from eternal issues.

The truth is, we have no ultimate control over our moments or the length of our time in this world. We cannot plan a long life for ourselves, and we cannot predict the future. As eternity belongs to God, so does time. When Jesus told his parable of the rich fool (Luke 12:13-21), he drew a very familiar scenario. The context of this story was a typical day in the life of the Lord Jesus Christ. People constantly pressured him to heal their hearts, teach them truth, and show them a miracle. Suddenly a man in the crowd said to Jesus, "Teacher, tell my brother to divide the inheritance with me" (v. 13). The Lord spoke to the man sternly, perhaps because, knowing human hearts, he could see the greed inside the one who made the request. "Be on your guard," said Jesus, "against all kinds of greed; a man's life does not consist in the abundance of his possessions" (v. 15). Here was someone caught firmly in the money trap, but he was also securely fastened in the minute trap, Satan's false conception of time. So Jesus told him a story to help release him from both of these traps.

Jesus told of a certain rich farmer who had fertile ground that had produced a bumper crop. He thought about what to do with this extra yield, since he had no room to store it all. The rich man said, "This is what I'll do. I will tear down my barns and build bigger ones, and there I will store all my grain and my goods. And I'll say to myself, 'You have plenty of good things laid up for many years. Take life easy; eat, drink and be merry.' But God said to him, 'You fool! This very night your life will be demanded from you. Then who will get what you have prepared for yourself?'" (Luke 12:18-20).

There are many lessons to be learned from this one parable. Not least is that the man was deceived by the devil. In planning to live a long enjoyable life of ease and indulgence, he had forgotten one essential thing: Our times are in God's hands. When God demands our life, it is all over! It was Moses who said, "Teach us to number our days aright, that we may gain a heart of wisdom" (Ps. 90:12). Moses lived many days. In this psalm he was praying for wisdom for every one of them. He was exceptionally conscious of his mortality. Are we? Listen to Moses' advice: "The length of our days is seventy years—or eighty, if we have the strength; yet their span is but trouble and sorrow, for they quickly pass, and we fly away (Ps. 90:10).

God's Word speaks a lot about time and what our attitude about it should be. The Bible uses comparisons to help us to see how few are our years, how frail is our existence, how momentary is our mortality. James uses the flowers of the field to teach us this lesson. He tells us that we will "pass away like a wild flower" (1:10). He had the same picture in mind as the mighty Moses, who prayed, "You sweep people away like dreams that disappear or like grass that springs up in the morning. In the morning it blooms and flourishes, but by evening it is dry and withered" (Ps. 90:5-6, NLT). I love flowers—all sorts, sizes, shapes, and smells. But I think the wild flowers of the field are among the most beautiful and delicate and definitely my favorites. It is no mistake that the writers of the Scriptures use them to picture the fragility of life.

So, while the devil is busy telling us that time is on our side and we have all the time in the world, God is telling us we are fools to believe him. One poet gives a compelling picture of this conflict:

> "Tomorrow," he promised his conscience,
> "Tomorrow I mean to believe.
> Tomorrow I'll think as I ought to;
> Tomorrow my Savior receive.
> Tomorrow I'll conquer the habits
> That hold me from heaven away."
> And ever his conscience repeated
> One word, and one only—"Today!"
>
> Tomorrow! tomorrow! tomorrow!
> Thus day after day it went on.
> Tomorrow! tomorrow! tomorrow!
> Till youth with its vision was gone,
> Till age and his passions had written
> The message of fate on his brow,
> And forth from the shadows came Death,
> With the pitiless syllable, "Now!"

Not one of us has tomorrow in hand. We only have today. So we are not masters of our own destiny. When our "number is up," as the saying goes, who can change it? Jesus asked, "Can any of you by worrying add a single hour to your span of life?" (Matt. 6:27, NRSV).

I remember learning that lesson at the tender age of five. Sitting on the steps of my parents' house in Liverpool, England, waiting for the air-raid sirens to summon us all to the bomb shelters, each night I wondered if this would be the night I would die! Living through the blitz wonderfully focused one's attention on what mattered, even the attention of a little girl. I survived, of course, but after the war was over and I entered my teens, I forgot in peacetime what I had learned at age five. Not until I found myself in the hospital at the age of eighteen did I learn the lesson of my mortality over again. On that occasion I was reminded very forcibly that I could not keep myself alive forever!

As I lay in a large ward in Addenbrooks Hospital, Cambridge, I found myself contemplating my companions. The girl on my right was all of seventeen years of age. Her mother never left her side except when forced to do so out of sheer exhaustion. She was watching her daughter's life ebb away. The young teenager had already lost a kidney when her remaining kidney began to fail, and, unfortunately, this was in the days before transplants. Those of us who were well enough talked about other things to try to keep our eyes off the activity around the bed on my right, but one night we all knew the battle had been lost.

Where is she now? I wondered desperately the next day. Her body was still in the bed, but she had passed away a short time earlier. Gone was the person we all knew, the girl who had lived inside that body. It was enough to jolt me into doing some serious thinking. Here I was with kidney trouble, too! To be sure, mine was not nearly as serious as the young girl's—she who had just, in Moses' words, "flown away"—but what if my problem got worse? I had no intention of flying away, but then neither had she! The really scary thing was having no choice about the matter. That harrowing experience prepared me for Janet, the girl in the bed on the other side of me, who witnessed to Christ and led me to him. So grateful that God healed me and had me out of there within the week, I went back to school believing he had indeed numbered my days, and apparently my number was not yet up!

As I have grown older, I have needed other dramatic ways to remind me of my temporary nature. One of the best ways God uses to remind me of my mortality is to make sure I must travel on an airplane a lot of the time! As I mentioned before, when we first lived in the States it was really hard for me to accept speaking engagements if I had to climb on one of those silver arrows to get there. I usually accepted the invitations but would board the plane in fear and trembling. When the flight attendant would say, "In the unlikely event of a water landing . . . " I would begin reviewing all I knew about the breaststroke. And talk about time standing still!

There came a point in my life, however, when I realized it was altogether inappropriate for me to be a gibbering wreck when the kind ladies who had invited me met me at the airport. After all, I had usually come to talk about faith. "Where's your theology, Jill?" my husband would ask me when, having arrived safely home, I spilled out my concerns to him. That is where I had to start. Did I really believe my days were numbered by God? Did I really believe I would not go to heaven one minute before I was meant to? Did I really believe God had a plan for my life—part of which included a time to die? Could I trust him with *all* my moments and my days, including that? I finally decided he was totally trustworthy and that I would trust him. After all, he had trusted me to trust him with my life and my death! It got easier after that. God worked in my life and overcame my fear of flying, basically by helping me sort out a solid theology of time. And he still keeps me on airplanes a lot, just to keep me depending on him!

One of the wisest of human beings wrote about a right attitude to time and urged us, "Remember your Creator in the days of your youth" (Eccles. 12:1). I became exceedingly grateful for the gift of life, physical and eternal, and now I have no problem remembering him. If we live like this, I am discovering, we will have no regrets in our old age.

If the devil sees that people are trying to get a right perspective on time and eternity and to acknowledge their mortality, he tries to distract them. "What will you do with your time?" he asks us. "If you only have so little of the commodity," he suggests, "why not forget your Creator and live it up! God is loving and kind," he says condescendingly. "He's bound to forgive you when you get up there." This was the essence of the thinking of the rich fool in Jesus' parable. Having fallen for Satan's con game, "Soul, you have many years laid up for you," he planned to begin to enjoy every one of them.

James addresses this same temptation in his letter:

> Now listen, you who say, "Today or tomorrow we will go to this or that city, spend a year there, carry on business and make money." Why, you do not even know what will happen tomorrow. What is your life? You are a mist that appears for a little while and then vanishes. Instead, you ought to say, "If it is the Lord's will, we will live and do this or that." As it is, you boast and brag. All such boasting is evil. (4:13-16)

We are a *mist,* not a must. James points to the brevity of life not only to give us a sense of the awesome nature of God, but also to give us an incentive to appreciate the few moments we do have and to use them seriously, wisely, and well. It is God's will, not ours, that matters in the matter!

We live in a very pretty little town in Wisconsin. Our condominium is on a small lake, and our kitchen window looks over this beautiful little piece of God's creation. Most mornings, if I am up early enough, I can see a mist shrouding the surface of the water. Usually it only takes the time needed to make myself a cup of coffee before the mist is gone. If I really counted the moments of the days God has lent me, and truly believed my life is but a mist, I have no doubt whatsoever that I would take greater care planning my schedule!

Scripture is replete with other beautiful images to help us get time in correct focus. Our earthly life is spoken of as a shadow: "Like a flower, we blossom for a moment and then wither. Like the shadow of a passing cloud, we quickly disappear" (Job 14:2, NLT). The worth of a shadow is in the substance that casts it, for it cannot exist on its own. The substance of our life *here* is eternal life *there.* Drawing on another analogy, Job says, "My days are swifter than a weaver's shuttle" (7:6). Those of us who have ever watched the speed of a shuttle in a skilled weaver's hand get the point. When we have finished our short lives, the tapestry woven by our actions will be displayed for all the world to see.

Then again, life is likened to a sprinter's race. Paul told the Philippian believers to "hold out the word of life—in order that I may boast on the day of Christ that I did not run or labor for nothing" (Phil. 2:16). Most of us run life's race as if it were a marathon, not a sprint!

Life is also depicted as a sigh: "We are like a breath of air; our days are like a passing shadow" (Ps. 144:4, NLT).

> My life is like a *shadow,*
> My God, reality,
> The substance of my soul
> And only hope eternally.
>
> My life is like a *shuttle,*
> Swift to weave the strands
> Of trivial moments spent in
> Filling all the world's demands.
>
> My life is like a *sprinter.*
> Too soon the line is reached.
> And God asks me for my response
> To all that I've heard preached.
>
> So brief and fleeting are my days,
> They pass just like a *sigh.*
> Yet God says they're important,
> And I'm not to question why.
>
> He doesn't give me more than these
> Few days to worship him.
> Perhaps he knows I'd use them
> For my selfishness and sin.
>
> And so my minutes, counted by
> The angels up above,
> I've chosen to be filled with songs
> Of joy for him I love.
>
> He's the substance to my shadow,
> The hand that weaves my story,

And the One who gives me breath
To reach the finish line in glory.

The minutes of the Master
Are precious worldly time
That shall be filled with Jesus,
Who's my reason and my rhyme—

My rhythm of sweet music
And the hope of all that's real.
So help me watch the moments
That the devil loves to steal,

Lord, save me from the minute trap
And from presumption cheese.
And teach me how to live for you
And not the way I please.

—J.B.

What, then, is the right use of time and the right attitude toward it? Undoubtedly, the right focus on time comes when we regularly use some of it to develop a relationship with God. "When," you might ask, "do we begin this relationship?" The answer to that is *Now.* Paul says, "Right now God is ready to welcome you. Today he is ready to save you" (2 Cor. 6:2, TLB).

There is one thing above all others that must be done in the time span allotted to us: We must make sure we take time to be saved! Whatever else we do or do not do, we need to spend some of our borrowed moments on our salvation. If our lifetime is the only chance we have to settle the issue of how we will spend eternity, then absolute top priority and attention must be given to this matter. The word *saved* may sound a little old-fashioned, so let me explain the term . . .

The Bible tells us we are all sinners (Rom. 3:23). No one on earth is sinless. Who has never sinned? Only Jesus Christ. Sinning is coming short of God the Father's expectation of us. And what is that? God expects us to measure up to his Son Jesus' character and life and therefore be perfect. Christ is his measure of perfection. He is the only one who has ever been sinless and fulfilled God's expectations. A sinner is someone who is less than ideal, who comes short of godliness. And that has eternal consequences! Sinners need something to happen to them before they can live in heaven, in God's holy presence forever. They need to have their sins forgiven. Only God can forgive us—cleanse us and invite us to live with him. Our triune God has made that opportunity possible for us by his death on the cross in the person of Jesus. We must thank him personally for this sacrifice, which saved us from the consequences of our sins. When should we do this? *Now!* The Holy Spirit says to us, "Today, if you hear his voice, do not harden your hearts" (Heb. 3:7-8). Think carefully and think long about this. It is eternally important. Has there been a special day you made sure you accepted Jesus as your Savior and Lord?

If you are uncertain whether this eternal business has been taken care of, it is really very easy to make sure. Just use your own everyday words to tell the Lord you are sorry about all the ungodly things you have ever done. Ask for his forgiveness. Invite his Holy Spirit into your life. Then thank him for hearing and answering your prayer. Paul says, "If you confess with your mouth, 'Jesus is Lord,' and believe in your heart that God raised him from the dead, you will be saved. . . . Everyone who calls on the name of the Lord will be saved" (Rom. 10:9, 13). Paul does not say everyone who calls "might be saved," or that we will have to wait and see how it all turns out on judgment day. He says *will* be saved."

We only have today. Whether we like it or not, that is how it is. Even if we are in the prime of life, who knows what is round the corner of tomorrow for any of us? Time ignores youth's arrogance and obeys eternity's clock. *Now* is the right time to confess your faith! That is where the right use of time begins. Once you have made time to accept Christ, and he has accepted you as part of his family, you need to take time to develop your relationship with him. One of the ways you can do this is by practicing praise. In *Decision* magazine (January 1992), Billy Graham wrote, "One reason we should number our days and apply our hearts to wisdom is that the day is lost which does not add to our knowledge of God and His Word. In eternity's scale of values that day is lost which has no word of praise, no prayer of thanks, and no contact with God. Prayer and praise are not occasional notes played on the organ of life; they are pipes in the organ, and their absence means serious loss to the music of life. It means discord instead of harmony."

God gives us 24 hours in each day: 1,440 minutes. With that amount, even if we gave the Lord 20 minutes a day, we would have 1,420 left for everything else! By "numbering our days," the Lord intends for us to think prudently about a seventy-year life span, even though we cannot be sure how many of these allotted years each of us will have. A Christian should certainly make long-range plans, for we need to be good stewards of our precious fleeting moments. But this must all be done with the ever-present realization that God has plans for us. Our times are in his hands. James reminds us that we "do not even know what will happen tomorrow," so we "ought to say, 'If it is the Lord's will, we will live and do this or that'" (4:14-15). As we develop and cultivate a moment-by-moment dependence on God and a submissive attitude to his will, Satan's bait of pleasure or presumption is less and less appealing, and we can avoid his time trap. As one of my favorite hymns has it:

> Take my life, and let it be
> Consecrated, Lord, to thee.
> Take my moments and my days;
> Let them flow in ceaseless praise.
> —Frances R. Havergal

"But," some of you may ask, "what if I do spend time with God each day but honestly feel as though I may not as well have bothered? How do I make my minutes with the Master worthwhile for him and for me?" Let me suggest some essentials.

It is up to you to decide on the appropriate time and place for your daily talk with God and to decide about how long that conversation should be. (Some days, you need extra time!) Once you are in the appointed place, the first essential is to be quiet and "wait on the Lord." What does this mean? So often we spend all our time with God asking him for something. Somehow we have to learn the art of praying without expecting specific rewards. We must learn to listen to the Lord without requiring answers to our prayer requests—to just be happy to "be still" and know that he is God (Ps. 46:10). That is the first thing he wants us to learn. The

Holy Spirit does not come into our hearts to do his deepest work in the shallow area of our emotions. The Holy Spirit desires to do his deepest work in the deepest part of us, in our hearts, minds, and souls. Much of the time a disappointing experience with a devotional time has to do with our failure to feel God near when we pray. We reckon that if we cannot sense his presence, it makes no sense at all to spend time praying! Yet the Bible says, "be still" and *know*, not *feel*, that he is God. Some part of those precious prayer moments must be spent just "knowing."

Concentrate on some of the things you have learned about God from the Scriptures. Maybe you realize he is almighty. Not a little bit mighty—all mighty. Be still and meditate on that for a while. Perhaps you understand that God has revealed himself in his Word as a God whose eyes see everything. "Know" that for a few moments. You need to give yourself enough time to let that happen. Only when we stop spinning like a top and remain still can we truly "know" that he is God.

Reading a few verses of Scripture will give you some things to focus on. James mentions at least four things about God you could spend time "knowing." He says God "gives generously" (1:5) and keeps his promises (v. 12). In the same passage James tells us, "God cannot be tempted by evil, nor does he tempt anyone" (v. 13) and "Every good and perfect gift is from . . . the Father of the heavenly lights" (v. 17). What a wonderful image to spend a little silent time in "knowing"! I usually find it most profitable to read the Scriptures right before my time with God. Then my mind does not wander. One of the biggest problems with being still is that the mind thinks this a perfect opportunity to plan the menu for dinner, worry about finances, or even wonder what on earth you are going to wear for the church social! You do not need to read a lot of verses—just enough to chew on, to bear down on, to meditate on.

Another essential part of prayer is spending part of the time journeying around the world! If you were to go on a cruise to the Caribbean, a tour to the Holy Land, or a safari in Africa, it would take a lot of money and perhaps fourteen days to do it. But you can visit the continents of the world during ten minutes of prayer. I remember someone passing on this concept to me when I became a Christian. I had always wanted to travel. Now I could go far away and not spend hours in an airplane seat to do it! But this travel has an eternal purpose that goes beyond the temporary benefits a physical vacation brings. I found I could be in China in the moment it took to think about it, and I could visit the homes of believers there who were being persecuted for their faith. I could spend a few moments asking God to strengthen these people and help them to endure and keep believing. Or within a moment I could be in Africa in the refugee camps, walking among starving children who were waiting for life-sustaining food from those of us who have material wealth way beyond our needs! "Lord, forgive us," I could pray. And he would make me see my part in alleviating their pain and suffering.

"But," you may object, "isn't there any time to be spent on me in my devotional time with the Lord? What about all my worries and troubles?" The truth is you have already spent time on yourself! Being still and knowing God gives you release from stress, peace of mind, hope, and confidence. Traveling the world in prayer, to develop a heart concern for a lost world and the Lord's people, makes you a healthier, outward-looking person—concerned less about "me" and more about "them." Praising the Lord surely turns a negative attitude into a positive one (good for ulcers, migraines, and heart trouble). And all of the above sets the stage for you to finally talk rightly to God about yourself and your own affairs!

And there is certainly full permission in the Scriptures to talk to God about yourself. James says, "Are any among you suffering? They should pray" (5:13, NRSV). However, praying about other people's troubles before your own brings your traumas into a proper perspective. As a sage's comment has it: "I grumbled when I had no shoes—until I met a man who had no feet!" When I have met someone with no feet in my prayers, my shoes become far less important than I had believed them to be!

"But how much of my twenty-four hours in a day does God expect me to share with him?" you may ask. All of it!! Prayer is a constant, a living awareness of God. Brother Lawrence said long ago, "Prayer is practicing the presence of God." Jesus said, "Set your mind on things above, not on things on the earth." That means we must spend all our moments walking with him, training ourselves to realize that since he is the Rock and each one of us his shadow, we are constant companions. But we are each also responsible to turn a few of those minutes of companionship into a more intimate, personal, and disciplined encounter. I need to do this every day, sometimes more than once or twice a day—but certainly at least once!

Daniel is a good example for us in this regard. When this mighty man of God prayed, he turned his face toward Jerusalem three times a day. The Scriptures say he was richly rewarded by visits from angels, visions of God, and victorious answers to his prayers beyond his wildest dreams! This man was willing to endure a lions' den rather than forsake his holy habit. Would we be so faithful? There must be a *must* about our mind-set and not a *maybe.* Our words and actions must say doggedly, "I'll be there, Lord. I promise I will not neglect the great salvation you have given me." How essential are these "essentials" in your life? Perhaps some of us need to start making up for lost time!

Of course, Jesus is our supreme example of the proper use of every moment. He had only half the usual allotted time span of a human being before his "weaving" was cut off the loom, his race run, and his breath returned to the One who gave it. Only a short thirty-three years! But just look what he accomplished—the redemption of the world!

We need to remember, however, where most of Jesus' moments on earth were spent. Jesus regularly visited his place of worship, the synagogue. But he spent many other hours with his family in Nazareth, at his carpenter's bench, and otherwise dealing with his family's concerns. This was how God wanted him to spend his early years. Jesus was able to say, "I always do what pleases him [the Father]" (John 8:29). Jesus' public ministry lasted only three years, but his private ministry lasted as long as he lived as human being. For him there was no difference between the secular and the sacred. It was all a question of where God wanted him and what God wanted him to be doing at any given moment. We might take a strong hint from this that making the best use of our time does not mean we live in church!

Jesus always lived out his minutes according to God's clock, not any human clock. This started with his birth. Scripture says, "When the time had fully come, God sent his Son" (Gal. 4:4). He was born at the right moment, and throughout his life he reminded his disciples, his family, and his friends, "My time is not yet come." He left us in no doubt that he was working according to a divine timetable. He was also crucified "on time," but so, too, was he resurrected!

David had the same sense of destiny. He said to God, "All the days ordained for me were written in your book before one of them came to be" (Ps. 139:16). When we get around to realizing that every one of our days is *ordained*—that is, set aside for God's use and purpose—even Monday mornings will look different. In fact, Monday will feel like Friday! Here, too, we can take the Lord Jesus as a model. God had it on his calendar that for thirty years his Son should live in a carpenter's shop in a little country town. There he was to attend the village synagogue and school, earn a living, and participate in the social life of Nazareth. He would have watched the farmers sow their seeds, enjoyed the religious festivals, and even experienced the horror of seeing Jewish victims crucified by the Romans at the side of the road. There was no such thing as an ordinary day for Jesus, even though it might be filled with ordinary things. Each day had extraordinary significance for him because he believed all his days were ordained by God. So it should be with our days.

Just as surely as God had a heavenly agenda for his Son Jesus, he has one for each of us. Every day of our lives, God writes down what he has in mind for his children on a clean white page of eternal history. The art of living as a believer is to come to the end of each day, see what your life has written on that page, and ask God if it matches his plan! Fulfilling God's plan is not just for pastors, missionaries, and Sunday school teachers. It is for laypersons like you and me and it is meant to happen in every one of our days! One of the first hymns I learned as a new believer went like this:

> All my days and all my hours,
> All my will and all my powers,
> Shall be thine, dear Lord.
> Shall be thine, dear Lord!

All our days–not just some of them–are his, but the frightening choice we have before us is whether to run our lives by our own timetable. We can do this if we will, or we can link up with the mind and heart of God and discover what he wants us to do with our days on earth.

This does not in any way mean we are to spend all our time with our noses in a Bible or singing psalms or praying. God has undoubtedly ordained all sorts of seemingly "nonspiritual" things for us to do. A great variety of experiences normally falls into the category of things that God expects us to accomplish. The writer of the book of Ecclesiastes says that there is a time and season for everything (3:1). He also says that God has put eternity in our hearts (3:11). That means there should be a sense of eternal things permeating everything we think and do and are! Since God makes "everything beautiful in its time" (3:11), there will surely be a beautiful sense of timing in our lives when we synchronize our spiritual clocks with God's. The whole of life becomes valuable and purposeful when we live our days for him, in whatever context we find ourselves.

I remember seeing my mother-in-law washing the dishes as if her life depended on it. Above the sink hung a plaque with these words: *Divine service conducted here three times daily!* (*Divine service* is the phrase used by the Church of England to announce their worship times.) I smiled when I saw that, knowing that my mother-in-law lived all her moments and days for Jesus. She would cook as if Jesus were going to eat the dinner she was preparing. She would shine shoes as if he were going to put them on. And she would dress daily as if Jesus were coming to visit! Eternity was in her heart; it permeated her time and motivated all her activities.

So how does this all work on a practical level? How do I avoid falling into traps such as the temptation to get so busy I can neither be blessed or be a blessing? How do I avoid ending up at the close of the day with a whole lot of regrets about how I have spent my God-given time? First of all, I take time to be "holy," to develop my personal relationship with the Lord. I sit at Jesus' feet and learn from him every day, however busy I may be.

Many of us remember the story of the time Jesus visited two sisters who were equally beloved of him but who represented two different kinds of Christians. Martha, the Scripture says, "was distracted by all the preparations that had to be made" (Luke 10:40). She loved the work of the Lord more than the Lord of the work! Although she was very busy serving him, this was not as he wished. At that particular moment, Jesus wanted her to be still, not frantic—worshiping, not worrying. "Martha, Martha," he said, "you are worried and upset about many things, but only one thing is needed. Mary has chosen what is better, and it will not be taken away from her" (v. 41-42).

Mary represents the Christians among us who make little pools of stillness in the middle of their busyness and take time to find out just what it is Jesus wants them to do. Every day, you and I can choose whether to be a Martha or a Mary. For those of us who love doing rather than being, it will be very hard to change our attitude. But change we must if we are to fulfill his plans for us and be fulfilled ourselves. Martha, for all her busy serving, was worried and upset. There was no peace in her heart. Jesus rebuked her *worrying* about her activity, not the activity itself. When we are in the right place at the right time, doing the right thing as far as the Lord is concerned, there will be peace and serenity inside of us. So the first thing to do is to stop so much *doing* and practice *being* a child of God. Make it a top priority. As you spend time in prayer about your plans, dreams, and activities, and ask God to guide you, he and his Word will give you principles and pointers to help you understand your daily place and actions. For example, we are not to leave God out of the reckoning when we move, change our job, or do our business. We should listen to him. We should, as James tells us, say, "If it is the Lord's will, we will do this or that."

When Stuart and I got married, we put our time into God's hands, and he put his will into ours. For three years we worked in the secular world—

Stuart as a banker, me as a teacher. That was what God wanted us to do! Then God's timing called for us to serve a youth mission. That was what God wanted us to do! So we moved from the city to the country. Ten years later, God's clock struck the hour for us to uproot, move across the Atlantic, and take the leadership of Elmbrook Church in Milwaukee, Wisconsin. That was what God wanted us to do! Twenty-four years later, we are still here and for one reason only: That is what God wants us to do! God brought us here, and until he leads us out as surely as he led us in, we will stay and do our best to fill our days with praise and service.

Study Guide: The Time Trap
For Personal Growth and/or Group Discussion

1. Make a list of your present priorities. (Be honest!) Then rework them according to your conscience. *5 minutes*

2. Discuss with family or friends the problems you have with Satan's time trap. *5 minutes*

3. If you have had "a day of salvation," share your personal experience with someone, or meditate on how it has changed your life. *10 minutes*

4. Read Psalm 90. What do you learn here about the following? *10 minutes*

    (a) Moses' attitude toward time
    (b) God's attitude toward work

Prayer Time   *10 minutes*

1. Reread the poem on pages 92 to 93. Which picture of life (shadow, shuttle, sprinter, sigh) strikes you and why? Pray about what God wants you to see and understand from this picture.

2. Pray for people who need salvation now. Pray for people who are "saved" but who are wasting time.

Pray for missionaries and all who are trying to further God's kingdom in our time.

3. Perhaps you are in God's waiting room. You feel suspended in "time." Try to believe God does everything right, and on time. Tell him you will believe and leave all your anxious thoughts with him.

5

To Live for Self or for the Spirit

The Morality Trap

One of the recurring themes of James's letter is wisdom (1:5-8; 3:13-18). A note in *The NIV Study Bible* on James 1:5 says, "Wisdom is not just acquired information but practical insight with spiritual implications." It is the wisdom that Solomon, probably the wisest man who ever lived, wrote about forty-one times in the book of Proverbs! It includes the idea of "skill in living—following God's design and thus avoiding moral pitfalls" *(NIV Study Bible* note on Prov. 1:2). The apostle Paul called Christ "wisdom from God" (1 Cor. 1:30, cf. Col. 2:3) and prayed that believers receive the Spirit of wisdom (Christ) so that they might know

God better (Eph. 1:17). We need God's wisdom—
that is, knowledge or insight that lies outside our
own human understanding—for all sorts of life's
choices.

Not long ago, some friends and I were having
coffee together. "I need wisdom to know what to
allow my teenage children to do," confided a has-
sled mother of two lively teens. "I need wisdom to
know if I should go back to work while I still have
two kids at home," worried another young mother.
"I need wisdom at work," chimed in a single
woman. "When everyone is talking about gays in
the military, I never know if I should give my opin-
ion." "And I need wisdom," added another friend,
"to know what to do with Dad now that Mother
has passed away. He shouldn't be alone, but he flat
out refuses to go into an elderly-care home!"

It is scary when you are not sure your kids are
making the right choices or you wonder whether
you are making the right choices for them. If, as a
parent, you are too strict, you might alienate your
children. And if you are too lenient, they might get
into trouble that they could have avoided if you
had stuck to your guns! It is hard to know how
much to say in the workplace when you know you
have only a limited amount of influence and information. Hardest of all may be the task of making
decisions involving aging parents who now need
their own children's guidance and support.

All my friends had difficult dilemmas, but they all
needed the same commodity—the wisdom that is
knowledge learned from God. Knowledge on its
own is simply an accumulation of facts. Wisdom is
knowing what to do with those facts once they have
been gathered. My friends had gathered as much

information as they could, but they were asking God to make them wise beyond human knowledge and experience.

With our limited capabilities, we cannot get the divine perspective on life unless we ask the Divine One to give it to us! "Good things" may not be the greatest things for us in the end. How to know? James tells us that we who know the Lord can ask the God of generosity to give us the gift of his wisdom to choose aright, and that God will not find fault with us for asking (1:5). But we must ask in full faith that he will guide and help us in our confusion. We can put our hand into the hand of God and be fully confident that he will not lead us up a blind alley! James described the person who doubts whether God is trustworthy and questions his integrity as "a wave of the sea, driven and tossed by the wind . . . double-minded and unstable in every way" (vv. 6-8, NRSV). Like a ship in a storm, this person is about to capsize!

When my husband was in business, we began to sense that we should at least investigate the possibility of Stuart's laying down his very promising career and offering our services to a youth mission. We took at least a year gathering information. We talked to people who knew us very well and could be trusted to give us good advice. We looked into several Christian missions at home and abroad, became familiar with their workings, and began to make a list of pros and cons for each opening for Christian service as it came along. Above all, we prayed hard for wisdom and got others to pray for it on our behalf. We asked God to help us find pieces of the puzzle that were still missing. We asked as best as we knew how for his direction, and we asked him not to let us make a mistake.

I remember Stuart saying to me, "Let's thank God in advance for what he's going to do for us. He's far more anxious we find the right thing to do than we are. He'll be delighted to show us which way to go!" We realized we had to ask in faith and not doubt his goodness. We needed to trust his generosity of Spirit and expect him to point the right way.

God did show us exactly what he wanted us to do. He helped us make wise choices at the right time and in the right manner. His gift of Christ— God's wisdom—was a precious treasure we valued and appropriated. Looking back, we realize he expects us to be bold and specific in our requests. After all: "You are coming to a King,/Large petitions with you bring."

Trusting God to tell us what we should do is all part of being in a living, loving relationship with him. He who is faithful to lay down our life plan will show us clearly the way to find it and give us the power to obey. Which brings us to the devil! He is bound and determined to keep us unstable or spiritually wobbly, and he will tempt us to be unwise about the ways and will of God. Which brings us to the morality trap! The devil, by seeking to get us to be immoral or amoral, attacks the faithfulness of God in our thinking and our faithfulness to God in our actions. Satan urges us to call on human wisdom instead of depending on God, because Satan wants us to find answers anywhere else but in heaven. But God expects us to be faithful and dependent on him alone. He is our Father, and we are his children. He is our Husband and we are his bride. The devil, however, baits the morality trap with "carnal cheese" and lures us into it, tempting us to doubt God's integrity and ability and to commit spiritual adultery.

Carnality is being double-minded about God. It is having second thoughts about the feasibility of trusting God to help us walk through the labyrinth of choices facing us today. Long ago and far away in a garden called Eden, the devil set the same morality trap for Eve. "You owe it to yourself to trust your own judgment about your affairs," he suggested slyly. "You don't need to depend on any outside agent. Be your own person. You can come up with a system of values and beliefs that you figure out all by your clever little self. They can even be 'moral' or 'religious' values if you like!"

That woman—the mother of us all—listened to Satan and was deceived into making a choice to eat forbidden fruit. A bigger problem was that she could not see anything wrong with it. The fruit looked so good. *It must be all right to eat,* she thought. And maybe there was nothing wrong with the fruit itself. The thing that was very wrong was to eat it when God had specifically told her not to! That was not very wise. In fact, it was very stupid indeed.

James tells us that when we are tempted today, we should recognize the source. He says, "When tempted," not if tempted. The devil has not died; he never takes a vacation and is actively recruiting our own sinful natures to accomplish his own ends. Says James, "But one is tempted by one's own desire, being lured and enticed by it; then, when that desire has conceived, it gives birth to sin, and that sin, when it is fully grown, gives birth to death (1:14-15, NRSV). There is something inside each of us that responds as readily to temptation as Adam and Eve did. Satan entices us, uses sights, sounds, and smells, and tests our moral strength to resist sin.

There are many, many things today that may be all right to own, read, participate in, join, or do. There may be absolutely nothing wrong with them in themselves. But the important question for a Christian is this: "Has God given me permission to involve myself in this particular experience or enterprise, or has he forbidden it?" It may well be a perfectly legitimate thing on its own, even a "right" thing, but you must be wise enough to ask God about it. If God tells you no, then for you it is illegitimate. "But Jill," you might say, "if something isn't wrong in itself, why would God say it's wrong for me?" The answer to that lies within our personal relationship with God and our implicit faith that a loving God will say no only if he in his infinite wisdom knows something we do not know. We must trust that he always knows the answer that is best for us.

Adam and Eve were told to be obedient to and dependent on God—to live within the rules laid down for them by their loving, giving Creator. Even if they did not understand those rules, God had assured them that his rules were for their ultimate good. One of those rules was to faithfully obey his instructions. The devil tempted them to question God's intentions in asking for such "blind" obedience. "How could God withhold something good from you if he really loved you?" he suggested cleverly. "If the fruit can make you feel good about yourself, Eve, what could possibly be wrong with that?" The devil cast doubts in Eve's mind that God really knew what was best for her. Satan offered to make her worldly-wise rather than God-wise, and she chose to listen to him. She took some of the fruit and gave some to her husband, although both of them were disobeying the specific instructions of God. So sin came into the world! Part of that sin was being double-minded about God's ways, something we call *carnality*.

Since Satan is not one bit creative, his tactics have not changed. He still casts doubts in people's minds about whether God can really be trusted with our lives and dreams. He also casts doubts about so-called Christian codes of behavior and makes them seem outmoded. For example, suppose a Christian woman falls in love with her boss, who is a married man. "God wouldn't want you to be unhappy," suggests the devil. "If it feels so good, it must be right. If that guy seems like such a perfect answer to all your dreams, what could be wrong with reaching for him?" We seldom stop to think long enough about such faulty reasoning. The devil is not stupid. He is not going to offer us a rotten apple, and we are too often duped by the wholesome look of the fruit he tempts us with. Anyway, "Everybody's doing it these days," we tell ourselves.

It is almost impossible to switch on the TV, pick up a novel, or read a magazine without being confronted with sensually seductive ideas. Packaged in a delicious manner, the carnal messages appeal to our "old nature." That part of us gets very excited about it all. We are "enticed," as James puts it. The problem is, most of those images or stories lull us into being complacent about carnality. We become people of two minds. One mind goes to church on Sunday; the other goes along with the thinking of the Monday-to-Saturday crowd. We begin to think that perhaps it is old-fashioned to regard marriage as a lifelong commitment. So we say, "Isn't divorce rather a good idea for those who made a genuine mistake but are now behaving like grown-up people and seeking a dignified alternative solution?" Or else Satan subtly suggests that we are not going to get along with our teenagers if we decide to tell them to stick to the sexual rules that God ordained (and we played by). Then we are tempted to believe it is time we got into line with modern culture and accepted the fact that most "normal" kids are sexually active. Even in church circles, loose morals seem to be generally accepted. Our God-given sexual appetite is under sophisticated attack, and what James calls "evil desire" looks so wholesome! Satan is "the prince of this world" (John 12:31), so he works on our passions and the passions of our kids.

Satan uses our passions and pride in "position" against us. For example, he tempts us with relationships that we have no moral right to accept (like being the future wife of a man who already has a wife!). But that "carnal cheese" is not the only one Satan spotlights for us. Status, too, has become golden in our western culture. Most of us who struggle to remain humble find it is not only money and what our dollars buy us that can bring us down. Part of a worldly or carnal mindset can even be found displayed in the church. There is plenty of self-pride in the body of Christ! We all know Christians who fight over opportunities and positions that give them visibility and glory.

After twenty-four years as a pastor's wife, I am

very well aware that as someone has cynically stated, "When the devil fell out of heaven, he fell into the choir!" Now, I do not really believe that, and I am sure you do not either, but you will probably agree there is often lots of posturing and jockeying for "position" in a choir. "Who is going to sing the solo for the special services?" a soprano may demand to know, asking for more than her words indicate. She really wants to know if *she* is going to be singing the solo. And if not, why not!

If the devil cannot catch us with this kind of bait, he tries to lure us with possessions that we can easily do without and that may well choke the spiritual life right out of us. As "prince of this world," he has the world's possessions to offer us! "Whatever takes your fancy can be yours," he assures us. From stocks and bonds to rare stamps—we only have to ask. The apostle John tells us that "everything that belongs to the world—what the sinful self desires, what people see and want, and everything in this world that people are so proud of—none of this comes from the Father; it all comes from the world" (1 John 2:16, GNB). These are the principles our modern world operates by. This is the lifestyle that Satan rules and the world he offers to us. To buy into it is to find ourselves caught securely in the morality trap.

The scary thing about "carnal cheese" is that Satan can make it look perfectly okay. He can even suggest that greed is moral, that it is the right thing to do to eat the food he offers. "Why, just think," his reasoning goes, "your boss may be rich, handsome, and have status, but he has had a miserable marriage. He has ulcers, his kids are a mess, and his business is suffering. Surely it's the right thing to do to rescue him from it all. Then his wife would be free to find a new and better partner the second time around. His kids would be everlastingly thankful to you for giving them a new and better mom, and his business would be saved because he'll be happy and more relaxed." The devil can make it sound as if it would be immoral not to do something about the situation. And you can almost believe it all, if you are listening to Satan-the-snake rather than listening to God.

A short time ago, while I was visiting one of our married children in Dallas, we stopped for an hour or so at a huge secular bookshop (a favorite thing to do). It was a great reminder to me of the face of our society at the present time. I found my way to the marriage-and-family section and could not believe the selection of topics. One book that was selling really well was *Get Rid of Him,* by Joyce L. Vedral, Ph.D. The subtitle was *Stay with the Wrong Man and You'll Never Meet the Right Man.* The chapter headings were things like "Get rid of him— if you're feeling trapped or dominated, if he's draining your energy, if he's more trouble than he's worth, if you're bored to death with him" and so on. No wonder we have a breakdown in family structure! I also noticed a book called *Family Values* featured on a special display table. *Good,* I thought, picking it up with relief. It was written by a woman named Phyllis Burk and subtitled *Two Moms and Their Son.* Looking around, I realized I was in the gay and lesbian section!

It took me a long time to find the Bible corner, which was also a mixed bag. Mary Baker Eddy was right in there with New Age cures, but there were a mere three or four shelves in all. All this in "Big

D," which would probably still consider itself part of the Bible Belt. What a wake-up call for the church, a signal to shout loud and clear above the din and confusion that marriage is a divine ordinance for the good of society as a whole and that we mess with it at our peril!

"Having a heart for God" means choosing to acquiesce to the will of God, not the dictums of the world. Anyone else who proposes a better set of rules to live by than God's is an impostor and is of the devil. God is love, but his heart was broken by the people he created. The book of Genesis tells us that when God looked down into a world full of carnal people munching on forbidden fruit, he was grieved:

> Now the Lord observed the extent of the people's wickedness, and he saw that all their thoughts were consistently and totally evil. So the Lord was sorry he had ever made them. It broke his heart. And the Lord said, "I will completely wipe out this human race that I have created. Yes, and I will destroy all the animals and birds, too. I am sorry I ever made them." (Gen. 6:5-7, NLT).

Humankind had chosen to become unfaithful and independent. As C. S. Lewis puts it, "The Great Divorce had happened and God was the injured party." Men and women chose to love the world more than the God who had made it, chose to worship the creature rather than the Creator of all creatures! "Their foolish hearts were darkened"; they had ceased to be wise and had in fact become fools (Rom. 1:21-22). Inclining one's thoughts toward "only evil all the time"(Gen. 6:5) means having a basic mindset of self-interest rather than God-interest, buying into the wisdom and ways of the world. This could be described as spiritual adultery. A "self-made" man or woman who boasts of his or her own accomplishments breaks the loving heart of God, who made us to recognize that we are God-made people who should worship him only (and serve our fellow human beings because of God's love in us).

So what does immorality, or spiritual adultery, look like? It may not always show itself in overt sin, for it will sometimes be dressed in very ordinary clothes. The only people who can fall into the morality trap are Christians. The world is well and truly trapped already, but believers have been "born again" and are supposed to have turned their back on the "Prince of this world" and to have sworn allegiance to the King of all creation. Therefore, walking into such obvious temptation is very stupid—but very common. I think it would be true to say that "carnal cheese" is consumed in large amounts by members of the evangelical Christian church with monotonous regularity, both privately and in full view of the world!

Let me define some terms for a moment. The Bible teaches that a "natural" person is someone who has been born only in the physical sense and has never been born again a second time, *spiritually*. Natural people do whatever suits their fancy, though they usually try to conform to the social mores that the world around them espouses. They may be extremely wise as the world counts wisdom, but pretty stupid as far as God is concerned. They are described in the Bible as being "of" the world.

ir world may be very pleasant. It may be that good things go on in the life of their community: ordinary things, everyday things. But because these "nice," normal things have no reference to God whatsoever, they are simply socially acceptable things.

When I was growing up, my world was exactly like that! It was a warm world, a fun-loving world full of nice, respectable, middle-class people who did not go to church and did not believe in hell or the devil. Even those who said they believed in a higher power believed in doing the best you could, treating people as well as was practical, and trusting in yourself to figure out the right responses to life as it came along. Trusting in God was considered to be a sign of weakness, since you would then not be self-reliant. Nice, normal events went on in my nice, normal world. My friends grew up, found jobs, and got married. They went out to eat at nice restaurants or whiled away their free time by a roaring fire and in happy company in pleasant, homey English pubs.

When the Bible describes the society that broke God's heart, it is speaking about people who were like the people working and playing in my nice world. They were "eating and drinking, marrying and giving in marriage" (Matt. 24:38). There is nothing wrong with any of the above—unless these things are done without reference to God, independent of his revealed will for us. There was nothing wrong with my world either, except our total disregard of, disinterest in, and disrespect for the Lord. Even a socially respectable life that leaves God out of the reckoning gives God angina! He calls it "only evil all the time." That is because while human beings look on the outside of a person, God looks on the heart and sees the attitude deep down inside. One dictionary defines *moral* as "pertaining to a philosophy that has to do with a particular system of principles or standard of conduct for right behavior." Because "man," male and female, is made in God's image, every one of us is able to make a distinction between what is really right and what is really wrong, whatever our social environment pressures us to believe.

It would have come as a total shock to me to be told in my early days that my harmless little living patterns were giving God a heart attack! But there came another time in my life when I was ready to be told the truth. Brought up by parents who believed in God though they did not attend a place of worship, I was taught as a child the Christian ethic—the Golden Rule—not only by word but by example. However, as I got older, their teaching was not reinforced by the company I chose to keep. My friends lived by a very different plan, and I fell into step right alongside them. True, my gang had its own set of standards (and they were not really bad as standards go), but as I rationalized my sin, called it "growing up," and threw myself into the party round at college, a deep vacuum opened up inside of me. No matter how hard I tried to chloroform my conscience, it began to wake me up in the middle of some self-indulgence and complain that I was not living as I should. Yet, you would never have noticed that any inner spiritual struggle was going on if you had looked at me on the outside. God, however, knows the difference between wrong and right, and since we are made in his image, we do too! When a Christian friend explained the facts of the gospel to me—that I was a sinner and needed a Savior—there was a great, glad response, a YES that sprang up from somewhere deep inside me. It made absolute sense. There was nothing required of me but to choose to be chosen, to quit being a fool and ask the only wise God to save me from my self-centered stupidity.

However, once inside the fold of believers, I discovered (as do all lost sheep who have been turned from going their own silly way) that the fight was far from over. As the hymn says, "Prone to wander, Lord, I feel it. Prone to leave the God I love." The natural person follows the urges and impulses of the "old" nature, divorced from God. Once the Spirit of God comes into our life, we are supposed to become "new creatures" led by spiritual impulses rather than natural ones. But I found out the daily choice to respond to the Spirit's leadings was mine. I could decide whether to live naturally or spiritually. So a "carnal" person is someone who has received the Holy Spirit and become a spiritual person, but is still living like a natural person. I found it was possible to live so "naturally" that my friends and family did not even know I had been born again! I soon recognized the trap—a trap that too many times I found myself walking straight into with my eyes wide open. Although I knew I should shun the "carnal cheese," it smelled so good!

I had only been a Christian for a very short time when a very exciting party invitation arrived. I was at a teacher-training college in Cambridge and had joined a dramatic society, quite a famous one called "The Footlights." I had been to just a couple of rehearsals and so was surprised and pleased to be included in the fun. The director was handsome and worldly-wise and had flirted with me a little, making me feel beautiful, intelligent, and sophisticated. Let me add that I had heard where most of the guests at those parties ended up—in the bedroom! I had continued attending other social events after my conversion, but I was suddenly conscious that I was at a crossroad. This particular party needed to be avoided. It was a very hard decision, especially since the director had put a little personal note on the bottom of the invitation, saying he hoped I would come. I knew, however, that my regular companions were well aware of all that went on at those parties. What would they think if their newly converted friend went to this one? I knew the answer to that, and praying for strength to do the right thing, I made an enormous effort and declined the invitation.

One of the big reasons it is very tempting to become a spiritual person but continue living like a natural one has to do with our close friends. Friendships play an incredibly important part in our lives. I remember that my problem, having been converted at college, was to figure out how much I should tell my friends so I could keep them. And it was not just a question of what to tell them either. My lifestyle had spoken volumes without my ever opening my mouth! Therefore, letting them see a change in behavior patterns was sure to give me away. It was very tempting to be carnal around my old friends, but spiritual around my new ones. This way I could be sure to keep them all! The devil loves to encourage us along this line of thought.

I remember my best friend finding the invitation I had declined. It was on my desk in my room when she popped in for a cup of coffee. "What's this?" she asked, picking it up and reading it.

"A party," I muttered.

"Oh, boy," she exclaimed, recognizing the name on the bottom. "So what are you going to wear?"

"I'm not going," I blurted out.

She stared at me in disbelief and spluttered, "What do you mean you're not going?"

"I-I-I can't—now—I'm a Christian—" I began.

She interrupted me with "Oh, don't give me that! I can't take a pious, holier-than-thou-friend. I think you're a fool!" And with that she slammed out of the room to tell my other friends that I had flipped my lid and was playing Joan of Arc! A little voice assured me that she was the foolish one and I had just done a very wise thing. But it hurt. It is hard saying no to "carnal cheese" when your friends think you should say yes.

The devil even suggested that I could become a little bit more "respectable" without rocking the boat. Not too much, of course, but enough to salve my conscience and keep my friends. The problem with this line of temptation, though, is that the world already accepts a code of morality without reference to God as God, so if we do not open our mouths and give God the credit for any noticeable improvement in our lifestyle, we run the risk of bringing attention and glory to ourselves rather than to him!

Fortunately, I learned early on in my Christian life that any life that is moral but excludes obedience to God—even though it might be a respectable life—is a morality trap. In fact, a "moral" life lived according to any set of principles other than those revealed by the God of Scripture is a life of "moral" sin! Without God, life is a morality trap. Being good without God is not being good!

Another point of confusion today lies in the different moral codes that are around us. Many women tell me they think one person's moral code is as valid as anyone else's—including God's. This philosophy leads to "everyone [doing] as he sees fit" (Deut. 12:8). The argument goes: "My right is as right as your right! What's more, I have the right to dispute, question, and refute your right!" So now we have exactly the same situation as Noah had in his day—people believing they have a right to believe and behave as they please, rather than realizing that as God's creatures in God's world, living by the grace of God for God, they should not be living as they please but rather in a manner that pleases him!

If Christians buy into this godless philosophy, they are not only trapped, but they can cause non-believers to reject such a wishy-washy kind of faith and cause younger believers to stumble as well. There is such a confusion of ideas in people today! A young man told me not long ago that he was living with his girlfriend. I knew the young man was a believer, so I asked him why, if he loved her, he did not go ahead and marry her. His answer was, "Oh, she's not a Christian!" He knew the Bible tells us we are not to be "yoked together with unbelievers" (2 Cor. 6:14), so he understood that he should not marry this woman. But he had fallen into the morality trap and felt it was okay to live with her according to the moral code of his friends. After all, everyone he knew was doing it! Being worldly-wise is not being God-wise, he discovered. He was caught in his own carnality.

Statistics are telling us that one in six of the kids on Christian college campuses are sexually active. These young people tell us they love the Lord but they do not go for their parents' old-fashioned, "Victorian" standards, especially where sexuality is concerned. Treating the Bible with selective indifference is not a very good idea! And it is certainly not God's idea.

The New Testament often refers to the Lord Jesus as the Bridegroom and the body of believers as his bride. So, too, in the Old Testament is God's relationship with his chosen people, Israel, described in terms of husband and wife. God uses the marital bond as a powerful image, knowing that everyone can relate to it. The prophets portrayed unfaithful Israel as breaking her heavenly Husband's heart, and Yahweh, the ever faithful spouse, as seeking reconciliation with his adulterous wife. Nowhere is this better shown than in the book of Hosea. Once Hosea is introduced to us as having an adulterous wife, this marriage becomes a touching parable of Israel's sinfulness and God's loving forgiveness. The wife's name is Gomer. She plays around, but Hosea loves her deeply and woos her back from her lover.

There are some beautiful parallels in this biblical story. God tells Hosea that all unrepentant Israelites are adulterers (Hosea 7:4). But God promises to "heal their waywardness and love them freely" (14:4). How will he do this? The words of God speak best for themselves:

> Therefore I am now going to allure her; I will lead her into the desert and speak tenderly to her. There I will give her back her vineyards, and will make the Valley of Achor

[trouble] a door of hope. There she will sing as in the days of her youth, as in the day she came up out of Egypt. In that day ... you will call me "my husband"; you will no longer call me "my master." (Hosea 2:14-16)

I will betroth you to me forever; I will betroth you in righteousness and justice, in love and compassion. I will betroth you in faithfulness, and you will acknowledge the Lord. (2:19-20)

So God promises to make the vale of trouble a door of hope! All of us can fall into sin. Perhaps you have sinned by committing physical adultery even as a Christian. Perhaps even *with* a Christian. Maybe you have broken your spouse's heart. Nevertheless, God in his mercy and renewing grace can bring you back to him, forgive you, and help you mend your marriage. Or do you think it is too late to help you get out of the mess? It is never too late to repent and return to God!

There is another scenario from which it is never too late to escape. Perhaps you have committed spiritual adultery. You have loved the world more than the kingdom of God, and the Prince of this world more than the Holy One who is King of heaven. Perhaps you have been reborn as a spiritual person but are living for all appearances as if you never had the experience of conversion at all. If this is true, know that your situation is breaking God's heart. Even as God promised Israel through the prophet Hosea, he wants to woo you back, forgive you, and reconcile you to himself. It is your choice. We can escape the morality trap if we want to! We need only open the door of hope and let God back into our lives.

From week to week I meet many women who have been in the Valley of Achor. This place got its name, "The valley of trouble," because of what happened there. *Achor* is another form of a man's name: Achan, one of Joshua's key soldiers. When Joshua was leading his men into the Promised Land, he told them not to plunder the belongings of any of the people, for God had told them they were to burn the cities and everything in them. On one occasion Achan saw "a beautiful robe from Babylonia, two hundred shekels of silver and a wedge of gold" and coveted them (Josh. 7:21). He was enticed by greed, by his old sinful nature. (I am sure the devil had run ahead of Achan and displayed the objects in a prominent place!) "I coveted them and took them," Achan eventually confessed to Joshua. "They are hidden in the ground inside my tent, with the silver underneath." Achan brought trouble to the beautiful land of Canaan that day. He had been caught in the morality trap—the lust of his eyes and his worldly-mindedness broke his covenant with God, causing no end of trouble for himself and his whole family. They were all executed. Achan had brought plenty of trouble to Israel, too. God told Joshua that he had allowed the Israelite army to be beaten because they had violated his covenant (Josh. 7:11). Even though Joshua had not sinned in this serious manner, Achan had, and God told his commander-in-chief that until the hidden sin was exposed, confessed, and put away, the people could not go on to conquer the land (Josh. 7:12-13).

After Achan and his family were stoned to death

for breaking God's covenant, the Israelites built an altar over their remains. "Then the Lord turned from his fierce anger" (Josh. 7:26). God is especially angry when we sin and try to hide it! He knows that hidden things will affect us—our families and our whole community, even our church. (If one bad apple is left in a barrel, it will soon bring rottenness to all the apples.) However, when we "confess our sins, he is faithful and just and will forgive us our sins and purify us from all unrighteousness" (1 John 1:9). The Valley of Achor then becomes a door of hope! God can restore. God can rebuild. He can and will forgive us and make us a blessing instead of a curse! The door of hope in our personal valley of trouble opens right in front of the cross of Christ.

If Satan can get us to love the world, he has rendered us ineffective as children of God. So he will try everything in his power to get us to live like a natural person instead of a spiritual one. James used a different term for what we call carnality. He said that anyone who questions God's faithfulness is "double-minded and unstable in every way" (1:8, NRSV). This describes carnality very well. Double-minded people cannot make up their minds. Because they doubt God's words, motives, and loving-kindness, they have wavering standards. Even after they become Christians, they cannot make up their mind to be the spiritual person they have become. Remember that James was writing to Christians who were in danger of falling into the morality trap. He says, "Therefore, get rid of all moral filth and the evil that is so prevalent and humbly accept the word planted in you, which can save you" (1:21). Can Christians actually get involved in moral filth? Oh, yes! The world has even witnessed some leaders of the church doing just what James warned against: "You adulterous people, don't you know that friendship with the world is hatred toward God? Anyone who chooses to be a friend of the world becomes an enemy of God" (4:4).

A divided heart can lead us into spiritual adultery. We are to understand that loving the world is just like loving a man who is not your husband! The world and all it stands for is that illicit lover. Jesus told us that marital adultery begins in the mind: "I tell you that anyone who looks at a woman lustfully has already committed adultery with her in his heart" (Matt. 5:28). Spiritual adultery begins in the mind, too. So we need to practice being single-minded in all our daily moments. As Paul puts it, we must "take captive every thought to make it obedient to Christ" (2 Cor. 10:5). And if it all begins in our thought life, we must choose to guard our minds. "Garbage in—garbage out" is a simple truth with a simple outcome. It depends in the end on which nature we are busy feeding.

The cuckoo is a bird common in England. It is large, ugly, and lazy. Not wanting to ruffle its feathers sufficiently to build its own nest, it finds a nest already completed and deposits its huge egg on top of the others. Then Mrs. Early Bird returns from hunting for worms and starts trying to hatch the eggs. It takes a big effort, but she succeeds and next sets about filling up the hungry mouths. Since a cuckoo's beak is twice the size of the others, guess who wins out! When the baby cuckoo is strong enough, he tips the other birds out of the nest and reigns supreme! What a revealing image this bird can be of our lives. If we have been born again, we have two natures inside us. The cuckoo stands for the flesh—the old nature, our carnal nature. Everything depends on which nature we are feeding; the one that is fed grows, develops, and finishes up reigning supreme! What do we feed into our minds? Do we nourish the spiritual nature or the natural one? The answer to that will be seen in our speech and behavior as we go about our daily lives.

The ways we feed our spiritual nature are very important. Just as we have three good physical meals a day, we need regular spiritual meals as well. Skipping one meal will not do us much harm, but eating only on Sundays will not do us much good! So we need to buy a readable Bible and read it often. Then we need to obey what it says. Above all, we need to keep very close to our faithful God, who will be both a Father and a Husband to us, protecting and providing for us moment by moment and day by day. This is the way we will learn to habitually reject the "carnal cheese" in the devil's morality trap!

Study Guide: "The Morality Trap"
For Personal Growth and/or Group Discussion

1. Read James 1:5-8. What is a double-minded person? Give some examples. *10 minutes*

   (a) Read James 4:4-10. (Verse 8 has that word *double-minded* again.) What is James's answer to being spiritually "adulterous," or carnal?

   (b) In Psalm 119:113, David says, "I hate double-minded men, but I love your law." What does the law have to do with being double-minded?

2. The parallel of Hosea's love for his wife and God's love for us has many lessons to teach us. *10 minutes*

   (a) Read Hosea 2:14-20. Which verse do you especially like? Why?

   (b) What do you learn here about the following?
   God
   Hosea
   Gomer
   The Valley of Achor
   Yourself

3. What one experience, person, book, sermon, or other source has most helped you to understand carnality? Share this with someone. *10 minutes*

Prayer Time   *10 minutes*

1. With a group, praise God for his Holy Spirit,
   which he gives us to help us lead spiritual lives.

2. Silently confess the sin of worldliness. Be
   specific.

3. Pray for the church, that it will be free from
   the sin of double-mindedness. Pray for the
   leaders of the church, that they will escape the
   morality trap.

6

To Develop God's Gifts or Waste Them

The Ministry Trap

J ames's words in the beginning of chapter 3 of his letter warn of a second trap in addition to the danger of misusing the mouth we studied earlier. He says that those of us who hold the privileged responsibilities of teaching and passing on scriptural knowledge must particularly watch out for what I call the "ministry trap."

The background to this passage of Scripture is quite interesting. Some people in the early church were pushing to be teachers. There was prestige attached to the position, so human ambition had come into the equation. James wanted his readers to know that those who wanted these assignments would be evaluated by other people and by God himself. With the privilege came such great responsibility and accountability that James warned, "Not many of you should presume to be teachers" (3:1).

Who were those teachers James was talking to and about? Undoubtedly, he was talking to leaders in the church, but also to laypeople gifted by the Holy Spirit to communicate—individuals given by God to the local body of believers (Eph. 4:11). These teachers were themselves gifts to the assembly of Christians. We can draw a contemporary application by saying that we who teach are we who pass on God's truth, whether as preacher, Christian educator, Sunday school teacher, home school teacher, Bible group leader, speaker, writer, discipler, or Christian mother. I think that covers quite a few of us! James is telling us that our motivation needs to be pure for this great task, which Paul refers to as teaching "these great truths to trustworthy people who are able to pass them on to others" (2 Tim. 2:2, NLT).

When I first became a Christian, the idea of each member of a church having a special ability to play his or her part was a new idea for me. Previously, I had not been near a church except for weddings and funerals, and my impression of the only church I knew was that the vicar did whatever ministry the congregation had hired him to do, while the people in the pews watched (and criticized until the poor man had a breakdown).

When I was led to Christ, however, I was immediately confronted with the doctrine of the "priesthood of all believers." The apostle John told the very ordinary folk he wrote to from exile on Patmos—Jews and Gentiles, bond and free, male and female alike—that He [Jesus Christ] "has made us to be a kingdom and priests to serve his God and Father" (Rev. 1:6). Christ had died and risen again, sent out his other self—the Holy Spirit—to form the mystical body of Christ—the church. He is the Head. We are the body, with each of us in our appointed place and each of us uniquely using our God-given talents and spiritual gifts for the good of the whole.

I was in training to be a teacher at the time of my conversion. Although teaching was an obvious talent I had before my spiritual birth, now my very profession had possibilities I had never dreamed of. Teaching in a downtown Liverpool school opened my eyes to the urban realities of the young people in that district. Their needs went far beyond the classroom curriculum, so my day did not end with the closing school bell. First of all, I set about being the very best teacher in the school. Then, outside school hours, I took to the highways and byways to find out what those youngsters in my class were up to!

As I began to care about them, argue the Christian faith with them, and teach them all that I as a young Christian knew myself, I discovered I possessed spiritual abilities to get their attention, keep their attention, and lead them thoroughly to Christ! My "teaching" became so much more than standing up in front of a classroom of kids and spouting off. Often it was a one-on-one experience and unplanned at that, just the kid and me sipping a cup of coffee and trying to keep out of the rain. Notably it was at such times that the realization dawned on me: God had equipped me to teach. Not just math, English, and poetry, but theology—a knowledge of

God that could well turn a young person inside out and upside down for the kingdom! How exciting and what a joy!

I found out, too, that it was vitally important to stay in touch with Holy God on a moment-by-moment basis if his truth was to be disseminated at the right time in the right manner to the right people. I have discovered that teaching can be as simple as leading a group of women into the Scriptures and helping them to apply the principles they find there to their everyday lives. It can be standing up in front of a Sunday school class of twenty or homeschooling a class of three. A teaching ministry is passing on God's knowledge to those lacking it, sharing what you know about him with others.

Some of the people James was writing to were apparently taking this privileged task far too lightly. They had, in fact, fallen into the ministry trap of pride. Seeing that pride always comes before a fall, James was concerned lest certain teachers bring their pupils tumbling down with them! Great joys await those of us who fit into the category of teacher, but so do great corresponding responsibilities. We should never hold our position lightly. James gives us the reason: "We who teach will be judged more strictly" (3:1).

The words of Jesus spring to my mind in this respect. The Lord told us, "If any of you put a stumbling block before one of these little ones who believe in me, it would be better for you if a great millstone were fastened around your neck and you were drowned in the depth of the sea" (Matt. 18:6, NRSV). Even as we teach others, we are to be busy teaching ourselves. Paul said to his protege Timothy, "Be a good worker, one who does not need to be ashamed and who correctly explains the word of truth" (2 Tim. 2:15, NRSV). In other words, we are to be diligent in our studies, and certainly we must be more concerned about studying than status.

But just how do we set about teaching ourselves? Very few of us will have the privilege of going to Bible college or seminary. Some of us have come to the Lord in our busy mothering years or even when we are a little bit older, so formal training may be out of the question. Still, we can all become our own teachers! First of all, we can teach ourselves to pray. Prayer is an absolute necessity if we are ever to teach anyone anything about God. We might be teaching others about prayer, but if we are not teaching ourselves to pray about teaching others to pray, those people will leave our class saying, "That was a nice talk," and never do much praying! If I spend an hour praying that people in my Sunday school class will pray, and half an hour stumbling through a simple talk about prayer, I stand a much better chance of having students learn to pray than if I spend no time on my knees and give a brilliant sermon on "intercession."

Second, I can teach myself the Scriptures. I need learning tools, and I need a little instruction from a pastor or lay leader on how to use them, but most of all I need to read the Bible for at least ten minutes every day, then let the Bible lead me to truth. I must open my Bible in a private place and read it with awe, expecting God's Holy Spirit to open my spiritual eyes to his truth, guard me from error, and speak to my heart. As I teach myself the Scriptures, I may not have any human being to help me, but the Spirit of Truth that Jesus promised to send into the world will explain all he wants me to know. I need to teach myself the Old Testament and the New Testament, too, because I need to learn all the facts and figures and matters that are important. If it is in the Bible, it is there because God wants me to read it, know it, learn it, understand it, and act accordingly. I must ask myself, "What am I doing that's stopping me from teaching myself the Scriptures?" Whatever it is, I need to take steps to stop a little of that "something else" to make way for the something he wants to tell me. His "somethings" are far more important than mine!

Finally, I need to teach myself to be like Jesus. Christians need to be holy, so we must talk to our unholy selves like a teacher and discipline our behavior. Do not say "I can't" to God. Be honest and say "I won't," but ask him to get you ready to start. Say, "Lord, I'm not willing, but I'm willing to be made willing." You cannot play games with God. Teach yourself to be transparent before him. Get on your knees and say, "Have a look at this, Lord, and tell me what you think about it. Tell me what to do about it, and tell me when to start." You cannot teach others about holiness unless you are in the school of holiness yourself. And that is a school from which you never graduate!

I have a theory that if we are determined to stay in touch with the Lord through all our moments, we will develop a holy awe as the truth handles us and we learn to handle the truth. We will then be in touch with ourselves and have a correct view of our size and importance, which will help us never to take ourselves too seriously. In contrast, if we push for the world's high places instead of the holy place of God, we stand a good chance of falling off our self-built pedestals and being judged by God into the bargain. James is pleading for humble purity rather than high position, a servant's spirit rather than a Pharisee's.

The Pharisees in Jesus' day loved to be greeted in the marketplaces as "teacher," and they made a practice of praying in prominent places so that their piety might be seen. Jesus roundly judged such actions as hypocritical and cautioned his followers to find a quiet closet rather than a crowded street corner for their devotions (Matt. 6:5-6). Those who were his followers were to take no notice of people's approval or applause, but to seek first and foremost to please God. Jesus, our Master Teacher, actually spoke to this precise point, using the example he set by washing his disciples' feet: "No servant is greater than his master, nor is a messenger greater than the one who sent him" (John 13:16). We can take this to mean that we, as Christians, are but humble servants of the Lord and must serve others in that spirit.

Besides the snare of pride, another ministry trap the devil loves to set uses numbers as bait. We need to be careful to concentrate on the people who are receiving our teaching and not on how many of them are receiving it. James must have remembered that Jesus spent the majority of his teaching hours training his twelve disciples, and that he constantly drew away from the multitudes to spend time with a handful of people. Sometimes we teachers get the feeling that if we do not have a crowd listening to us, it is not worth the trouble! We must not play the numbers game when we witness to God's truth.

As I have mentioned, when my husband and I

served a youth mission and were based in England, I was in the "mothering season" of my life. Stuart's extensive traveling gave me lots of free time at night once the three children were safely tucked into bed. We lived in a home on the grounds of the Youth Center—a huge castle set in the gorgeous English countryside—and I often longed to be actively participating in the work right in the middle of all that young life. Hundreds of young people came through the center's doors every week from dozens of countries, and the staff members were trying to cope but were stretched to the hilt. "If only I could teach," I complained to God, thinking of the large number of kids up at the center. "You can teach if you want to," replied the Lord. "Teach your neighbors about me."

I fully realized that my job was to nurture three busy little preschoolers at this time in my life, so I needed to stay put. How could I reach out to my neighbors, a collection of elderly women who lived around me in the valley? It was at this point in my wondering that I was reading through Isaiah and came to chapter 6. I was struck by the fact that rather than send his gifted prophet to huge receptive congregations, God sent Isaiah to people who would hear but not understand and see but not perceive, people whose obdurate hearts would remain the same when all his teaching was done (Isa. 6:9-10). Isaiah did not choose the people he would preach to. He let God do that. He said to God, "Here I am. Send me!" Seeing his example, I felt I needed to echo his words and set to the task.

I soon became aware that God wanted me to go to "the little old ladies" and not to the crowd up at the Youth Center. It was hard for me to say, "Here am I—send me to a few little old ladies," instead of "Here am I—send me to that hoard of kids," but in the end I managed to do so. For months, three elderly ladies and I studied the Scriptures together. One of them was blind, one was deaf, and the other had heart trouble! I looked at the Isaiah passage again and realized that these were my people as far as God was concerned. Months after we began, one little lady found the Lord, then another. We ended up with twelve very elderly, very committed Christian believers. They became the pray-ers and encouragers of a work that eventually reached many for Christ in that sleepy English valley. I learned then that if God has gifted me as a teacher and given me as a gift to his church, it is all to fulfill his purposes. I am to stay close enough to listen to my instructions and to be as willing to pass on the Good News to one person as I am ready to speak to a thousand. The numbers I reach are quite irrelevant; obedience is the thing that matters.

That lesson has stood me in good stead in these last years. In America one is tempted to believe, "If it isn't green and growing, it's dry and dying." But that is not true! Growth is not always the evidence of life. Sometimes a tree reaches the size it was meant to be. Then all that happens is the roots grow deeper!

James addresses another ministry trap when he says, "We all make many mistakes, but those who control their tongues can also control themselves in every other way" (3:2, NLT). Satan turns this around and attempts to trap us in perfectionism, which sometimes becomes false humility, a form of pride. "You're not good enough, bright enough, holy enough, to teach anyone else" the devil whispers in our ears. (It may be that he uses numbers or lack of them to discourage us at the same time.) If this is indeed our problem, we need to set our eyes on the Master and become "good enough," expand our minds, and work on being holy people. All Christians are to "go and make disciples of all nations" (Matt. 28:19). If we wait until we are perfect enough to do it, trained enough to do it, or rich enough to do it, we will never open our mouths. We must be growing and knowing and going somewhere all the days of our lives!

When I first arrived in the States, I was thirty-four years of age, fresh from a ministry with youth in Europe, and very excited about the challenge that lay ahead. Stuart and I had been called to lead a church in suburban Milwaukee. I had had very little experience with church work, church structure, church politics ... church anything! I had been unchurched in my growing years and converted as a student at college. After marriage I had joined a nondenominational mission that ran youth conferences, serving the church at large. Sundays, we had a worship service at the center, but I never officially belonged to a church fellowship until ten years or so after joining the mission. Then we chose to respond to a call from Elmbrook Church and emigrated to the States, and I became a pastor's wife.

Struggling with culture shock, I looked around me and saw highly trained, competent people doing what they did very well. In fact, I could not see anyone doing dumb things or struggling along learning a skill. It all looked so perfect! I was used to "muddling through." If a job needed doing, you put your hand to the task and did the best you could. Now I was faced with the "credential" requirement.

The feeling seemed to be, if you did not have the right credentials, you should not be doing the job. There was little freedom to fail, no credit given to natural ability or effort beyond the call of duty. It was a typical ministry trap.

I thought about this trap a lot and almost became caught up in it myself. As I worked alongside the women and college-age kids at church, I began to realize they were frightened of doing anything badly. It was catching. I, too, began to be scared of doing anything I did not think I could handle well. I talked it over with Stuart, who cheerfully responded, "If a job's worth doing, it's worth doing badly rather than not doing it! How do you learn to do something well if you don't start by doing it badly and practicing?" As James said it: "We all stumble in many ways" (3:2). The question I faced was whether I was willing to stumble visibly and badly in front of my new friends and congregation. I decided I would not fall for Satan's lure of "perfection cheese." I would try to respond to needs, do the best I could, and not wait till I could do something perfectly before doing God's work.

As I set about putting these principles into action, I discovered gifts that previously I had no idea I possessed. Insecurity can lead you to back off, especially when you look around and see people all around you doing things extremely well! The main credentials for ministry are a loving heart that wants to serve the Lord, and a willingness to learn as you go along. This especially relates to teaching. Nowadays, credentials are given a much-needed emphasis in many fields. But you do not need to have seminary training to pass on the knowledge you are learning about God by yourself. I certainly have put myself under a rigorous personal study program (never having had the chance to go to seminary), and I have discovered that the books, tools, and other learning materials are out there for me. But I do not wait till I am perfect enough in knowledge before I witness for Christ, teach my Bible-study classes, and respond to invitations to speak around the world. I do my homework and try to stay in touch with God. I hope to get better all the time.

Of course, no matter how hard I try to stay in touch with God, sometimes I will make a serious mistake and stumble. We all do that! But when we sin, we must repent and be restored and work extra hard at not falling into the same old sin over and over again. As we keep ourselves humbly available and accessible to God's cleansing Holy Spirit, we can continue to pass on truth to those who desperately need it.

Years ago, the youth group at our church put on a play in which the lead actor was a youngster straight out of the Jesus Movement. He was very talented. Two days before we were to present the play, he came to me and said, "I can't do this because I'm out of touch with God and have sinned." Indeed, the problem he shared needed attention. He had stumbled badly. "So you see," said the young man after he had recounted his concerns, "I am so imperfect that I cannot take the lead part. How can I be in this play and teach others through this drama when I have been such a fool?"

"Go over there," I told him, "and get into touch with God again! Then, after you have repented before God, put right what you can. Make your phone calls and do whatever else you need to do to make restitution. We all stumble in many ways," I reminded him. "Nobody's perfect. However, your responsibility is to be teaching others through the medium of drama, so you mustn't fall into the trap of letting the devil tell you that until you are perfect, you can't perform!" Fortunately, he took my advice and let God cleanse him. Humbled and renewed, this young man was ready to fulfill his teaching assignment and did it very well. I said thank you to James and heaved a sigh of relief!

If the devil cannot catch us in perfectionism he will change his tactics and trap us in other ways. James tells us we are to "keep [ourselves] from being polluted by the world" (1:27). Worldliness is being "me"-centered instead of God-centered. Because it involves both pride and false humility, worldliness has particular reference to the heart of the teacher. Any sin that comes between the Lord and those of us who minister in his name will pollute our hearts and render us ineffective.

One particular kind of pollution related to ministry today is materialism, which shows us that the devil's devices have not changed. On the eve of the Lord Jesus Christ's ministry, Satan offered him the world if he would stop doing what God had sent him to do. Of course, Jesus refused the bait, so Satan now concentrates his efforts on us! We should not kid ourselves, either. All the world's gifts, glamour, and glitter are appealing. However, as Jesus pointed out in his parable of the sower, "The worries of this life and the deceitfulness of wealth" can choke the seed in our lives (Matt. 13:22). Polluted land bears no harvest! Jesus also said this: "Make a tree good and its fruit will be good, or make a tree bad and its fruit will be bad, for a tree is recognized by its fruit" (Matt. 12:33). James echoes that thought: "Can a fig tree bear olives, or a grapevine bear figs?" (3:12). James puts the responsibility on us. If "we who teach" cannot keep ourselves from being contaminated by the world, the "seed" of God's Word within us will not produce the life of God in others through us.

Materialistic temptations come in many forms and many ways in ministry. For example, as a Christian speaker and author, I struggle to keep myself from being "polluted by the world." Paul tells us he did not peddle the word of God for profit (1 Cor. 9:18, PHILLIPS). As another translation puts it, Paul's "reward" was to "offer the gospel without charge" (NASB). What does this mean in terms of speaker fees, book contracts, and honoraria? I must struggle to hear the still, small voice of God in my professional life telling me where and when to speak and whether it is all right to accept "free will offerings." I pray a lot about not allowing materialistic considerations to contaminate my speaking and writing decisions.

Another form of materialism that can entrap those who minister shows itself in love of performance and prominence. If they are not careful, "up front" religious teachers and leaders can start to enjoy the limelight so much that they are blinded to the things that they need to be doing in secret. People with such public responsibilities must preserve balance between serving and speaking. If we have "up front" gifts, we must work hard on our serving graces. Satan knows we like to feel important in the world's eyes. To the poison of love of prominence, quiet service is the antidote. If I do something for God that everyone knows about, I try to do something for God in private that nobody knows about, something that balances my good words with good works! Not that all good works must be done in secret, but we can choose to do some of them for God's eyes alone. When we are busy serving solely for his sake, we are actively avoiding the ministry trap of self-promotion.

This balance between dogma and doing must also exist for the world's sake. After all, James points out, "Religion that God our Father accepts as pure and faultless is this: to look after orphans and widows in their distress *and* to keep oneself from being polluted by the world" (1:27, emphasis mine). Am I practicing what I preach and preaching what I practice, so that unbelievers can see a little of this Spirit-filled philosophy worked out in me? Scripture does not say that true religion is all words, and neither does it say that undefiled, un-polluted, unworldly religion is all works. James tells us, "Faith without deeds is dead" (2:26), so if my words are to have any effect on those I witness to, my works must be seen to underline and emphasize the truths I am passing on. If our words reflect our works (and vice versa), we can avoid the pollution of our souls. The devil prefers us unbalanced. "Why don't you be all works and no words?" he suggests, subtly baiting the ministry trap with the "busyness cheese" of over commitment. Yet, if we simply work our heads off for society's disenfranchised, those who see our good works may well glorify *us* instead of our Father in heaven! How will they ever know we are doing what we do because of God's com-mands and the grace and power of the gospel, if we never tell them so?

We need lots of God's servants demonstrating good works to the watching world, but the observers must also be told that these things are being done by the enabling power of a good and gracious God. We must show the world our faith by what we do, says James (see 2:14-17). This is what Jesus meant when he said, "Let your light shine before others, so that they may see your good works and give glory to your Father in heaven" (Matt. 5:16, NRSV).

Rosie, an elderly Christian woman, was once asked whose preaching she had been saved through. "Nobody's preaching," she replied. "Aunt Mary's practicing." I venture to suggest, however, that if Aunt Mary had not been able to articulate the hows and whys of her own good life and good works, Rosie would not have come to faith herself.

Effective leadership is a continual learning process. In the Western world, where Christian leaders are appreciated and affirmed and often adored, there are tempting traps waiting to pollute their souls and their ministries. Therefore, as leaders learn to lead, they must learn to lean—to lean on the One who will teach them to teach, show them how to serve, and keep them thoroughly balanced. The same principle applies to every believer! We may not all consider ourselves "leaders" in the usual sense of the word, but that is what we are. For we are commissioned as the Lord's disciples (Matt. 28:19-20) and expected to lead others to his truth.

I found out very early in my Christian experience that teaching required me to learn and lean on a regular basis. Being of a somewhat lazy disposition, I came to understand that having to prepare a "lesson" on a weekly basis for the same group of people was very good for me indeed. First of all, it had to be something new, which meant I had to learn something new. I also had to keep one step ahead of my class, not always easy to do when you have eager, hungry students. Second, I had to make it interesting, which meant it had to be interesting to me! I needed to dig, to read around the subject, to let the text come alive for me so I could make it come alive for others. This took time and energy, research and creativity. And all this work added up to learning-and-leaning time with God. The discipline was good for me, so I soon started to volunteer to teach somebody something somewhere more often. In the summertime, when Sunday school recessed, I would find someone who would meet one-on-one with me over my kitchen table, and we would study something together. All because I was learning to lean on God.

Being an effective teacher does not just mean you learn to lean on God for inspiration and strength. It also means you learn to lean on him for specific answers. Today's pupils do not sit silently in rows, passively absorbing your lessons. (In fact, in my experience that has never been the case!) They ask questions: hard questions but good questions. What to do? Lean. I love to be faced with questions that leave me flummoxed! I have learned to say, "I don't know, but I'll find out," or "I think I'm right in telling you such and such, but I'm not sure." Or I ask, "Does anyone in the group know the answer to this? I'm afraid I don't." Above all, I have learned to lean internally on God and pray silently, *Lord, give me the answer I should give.* Occasionally, answers have come that I did not know I knew. More often, I have gone away and done some research and come back the next week with the answer. One way or another, being a teacher pushes me to the frontiers of my faith and forces me to look to the God who is omniscient and who in his grace shares some of his knowledge with me for the good of others.

When people come to me (as they do quite often) and tell me, "I want to do what you do—teach in churches and large meetings," I look at them and think of James and his appropriate warnings. While some people are willing to be mentored or lead and have sweet, open attitudes, many others, like folk in James's day, "presume to be teachers." I first advise them to join a church, if they have not already done so, and begin to teach in the Sunday school. "No, no," they say, "I don't want to teach in the Sunday school. I want to speak to large groups, like you do." So I try to tell them how I learned—learned to lean—and that my apprenticeship was served teaching groups of two and three and sometimes five and six for years as I learned my trade. But they are not impressed. When I argue, "You don't start at the top," they want to know "Why not? Why not aim high?" Then I try to show how aiming high is aiming low. The way to up is down and the way to down is up! I tell them that in all my speaking and teaching, I try to balance whatever I am doing by meeting regularly with a small group of people and studying the Scriptures together. "Aiming high doesn't mean aiming big," I try to warn the overly ambitious. "Aiming high means aiming low at humility—seeking to have a Christ-like heart and attitude and being willing to start teaching a few willing learners!"

James gives us a most important clue to achieving balance in a ministry through a warning: "We who teach will be judged more strictly" (3:1). The key is in that little word *we*. That little word has a big meaning! James does not say, "I who am your teacher," but *"we* who teach." He is addressing the whole church, the body of which he is a part. In the little word *we* lies the key to controlling our carnal natures. There is no place for the maverick minister out there! The leaders of the church must lead, but they are only one part of the whole. The teacher is a "mouth," yes, but a mouth needs a mind and a heart to direct its speech. And where could the words of a mouth travel without the feet? Teachers must be accountable to every part of the body of believers, and especially to the Head, the Lord Jesus.

It is in the community of believers that the checks and balances are kept. James knew he was accountable to others. It was this aspect of the teacher's life that would above all else keep him out of the ministry trap! The respected teacher James submitted to the lesser-known members around him. Yes, he was the Lord's brother, but he had other brothers and sisters in the family of God. If he was tempted to be proud or have false humility, a brother in the church would lovingly rebuke him. If he was tempted to grow fond of his position and lord it over others, he would be brought into line by a Peter or a John or a Priscilla or Aquila. If he felt himself inadequate, he would be encouraged and affirmed by those he taught. And if he became unbalanced, a brother or sister would pray him back into right perspective on his ministry. "We who teach" must look out for each other and listen to each other, but we must also learn to listen to those we are teaching. In the body of Christ, one member is no more important than any other. In fact, Paul tells us that those members who have limited visibility or seem weak are to be held in more honor by the whole than the highly visible (1 Cor. 12:21-24).

The body of Christ is an essential framework for those who teach and lead in the church. Not only must the church as a whole affirm and confirm the gifts of all its members, but it must also make sure there are opportunities for those gifts to be exercised for the edifying of the whole body. Women with teaching gifts especially need to find a local fellowship of believers in which their gifts are put to use. I count myself in the category of "we who teach." I have teaching gifts, but there are those within the Christian establishment who would tell me that those gifts are not to be exercised within the church simply because I am a woman. I would take issue with that position. James did not say, "We *men* who teach." Both men and women, in harmony and mutual respect, are to be teaching God's truths so that others, too, can pass them on.

Not long ago, a lovely lady with obvious teaching abilities asked a pastor who would not allow her to use those gifts in an adult education class, "Why, then, has God given me those special abilities?" "So that you can submit and learn humility as you give up the gift of your teaching," he replied. (This is not as uncommon a position as you might think!) I cannot imagine a God who would be so unwise and unkind as to gift a member of the body with speaking abilities that could be used in the building up of the body—and then would tell that person to keep her mouth shut to learn what humility and submission were all about! I do not believe the

Scriptures teach that women cannot or must not teach. Preachers must preach, teachers must teach, singers must sing, helpers must help, administrators must administrate, organizers must organize, evangelists must evangelize (see 1 Cor. 12:27-31). Why else would they be a part of the body?

Years ago, my husband was invited to write an article on this topic by *Moody Monthly.* He wrote about the Lord Jesus' warning that we must not bury our talents. In the article, Stuart posed the question, "What will God say to those of us in the church—often men who are in control—who bury other people's talents?" (namely women's). God is the One we are all subject to. He is the Judge. As women with speaking and teaching talents are encouraged in the context of the church to exercise their God-given gifts in the edification of the body, every part of it will become stronger and bring greater glory to God.

We who are teachers, men and women alike, must do our part. But we must do so in a spirit of humble submission to one another and of obedient dependence on the One who came to teach us how to so minister that men and women find the way to be forgiven and take their own place in the plan of redemption. James says we will be "judged more strictly," which means we are especially accountable to others. We should think of that accountability in two ways. We are accountable as to *how our gifts are exercised* and also as to *the extent of our development of our gifts.* We need to exercise those gifts in full measure!

I am so grateful for the blessing of being married to a man who has held me accountable to do both of those things! It is an added blessing to be serving a local body of believers (and many in the world-wide church) who have held me accountable as to how I use my gifts. Far more than that, they made a place for me and insisted that I use them! It has been the fellow believers, especially the men, in my life who have affirmed, confirmed, and reaffirmed my teaching gifts. Because of these people, there will probably be many more people in heaven! In the end, of course, we who teach will be judged and held accountable by God.

Study Guide: The Ministry Trap
For Personal Growth and/or Group Discussion

1. Read Ephesians 4:1-17. According to this Scripture: *15 minutes*

   (a) Who gifted the gifted?
   (b) To whom were the gifted ones given?
   (c) Why?

   For discussion: Who falls into the category of "teacher" in the Christian church today?

2. Review the ministry traps that we must avoid. *10 minutes*

   (a) How can we avoid "teaching others and not teaching ourselves"?
   (b) What practical steps can we take to "learn and lean"?
   (c) How can we stop "the world" from polluting our teaching ministries today?

3. If one of the keys to avoiding the ministry trap is accountability, how can "we who teach" make sure we are accountable? *5 minutes*

4. If you are a woman with teaching gifts, are you being affirmed and confirmed by the body of believers? If not, what can you do about it? *5 minutes*

Prayer Time   *5 minutes*

1. Pray for teachers who are tired or discouraged, and also for those who are ignorant, dominant, proud, or bossy.

2. Pray that churches will train their laypeople to do the work of the ministry according to their gifts.

3. Pray for all who teach and train our children.

7

To Persevere or Protest

The Misery Trap

Having started his letter dealing with trials and troubles, James ends on the same note. He discusses the "poor me" syndrome, the misery trap that the devil sets, hoping to get us weeping and wailing and gnashing our teeth so hard that we forget our lifeline. We forget that we can and should be calling on the eminent Lord who promises to be with us, stick with us, deliver us from trouble, and send us out into the light of a brand-new day. If the devil can lead us to be sorry enough for ourselves, we will never be sorry enough for others, and our focus will be diverted from one of the main reasons for our being. The devil knows that once our own true healing begins, we will step over the line from being sorry for ourselves to being sorrier for someone else.

I have a good friend whose husband walked out of her life after many years of marriage. She was devastated. For months she sank deeper and deeper into despair. Then one day she managed to search out a church (ours) and look around for an entry point. Our church is very large, and it seemed totally overwhelming to my friend. "I've got to find somewhere to serve," she thought desperately. "I know—I'll volunteer to help in the kitchen." And she did. She began to work hard at getting to know people while doing the most menial jobs. She was a schoolteacher by profession and a good manager by nature. Soon she had the whole kitchen area organized and began recruiting and training other helpers. Most important of all, in the course of serving with others, she discovered people with grievous heartaches, most of them much more serious than her own. She began to listen, weep, care, and minister out of her own pain. So she began to heal. In her own words, "I stopped asking for help and became a helper. That's when my recovery began!"

James reminds his readers to "be patient," for Jesus is not only there for us in spirit, but he is also coming back to earth! (5:7-8). This must have been a unique thought for James, since it was his half-brother he was talking about. To receive someone back from the dead would be highly unusual, to say the least, but to receive that person back as Lord and King of the universe and Judge of the earth (when you had lived with him in Nazareth for the best part of thirty years) would have been far beyond unusual for James. Yet he and most other early Christians believed that Christ would come, and soon. Therefore, daily living needed to be ordered accordingly. I am quite sure James would have spent hours listening to the apostles' recounting of Jesus' words about his second coming, and asking them questions. James must have heard of Jesus' promise that if he left his followers, he would come back for them (John 14:3). He would have realized that though life would be going along as normal, the Lord would return and surprise the world at a time when no one would be expecting him (Matt. 24:36-44).

Perhaps James had memorized the Lord's words, "So you also must be ready" (Matt. 24:44), and was standing on tiptoe, as it were, ever expecting the great reunion. Of one thing James was sure: The Lord is coming back, and as surely as a farmer knows his land will yield a harvest, we can know it will happen (5:7-8).

Because I had grown up rather illiterate biblically, I had no idea about the second coming of Christ. I had never heard it mentioned in my early years as far as I can recollect, even though prayers and creed were recited in school, and Scripture was taught by law in the classroom. But upon becoming a Christian, I began to devour my Bible, and the second coming was one of the things I found there that I had never noticed before.

Shortly after I became a believer, my boyfriend invited me to attend May Ball at the university. This was the social event of the year at Cambridge and quite an exciting and lovely occasion. After a couple of dances, the young man said shyly, "Jill, I have to tell you something. I went to a meeting and heard Christianity explained, and I gave my life to Christ."

I stopped in shock, right there in the middle of the dance floor. He was a rather wild young man (as I had been a rather wild young woman), and I could not believe it. He looked decidedly nervous until I burst out with "Oh, how wonderful! I became a Christian, too!" Then, standing dead-still in the middle of the dance floor, we both began to talk at once. The people around us gave us curious looks, but we did not care how it seemed to them. "Jesus Christ" was on our lips, and all our newfound faith and love spilled out, creating a bond far closer than any we had known before.

"Do you know he's coming back?" my boyfriend asked me.

"What do you mean?" I answered, astonished.

"Someone at the meeting I attended said that he's coming back again to earth."

"Like another baby?" I wanted to know.

"I don't know," he said, "but I have a Bible in my room that might help."

"Let's go and read it and see if it tells us how and when," I suggested. And so we spent the first part of that May Ball sitting in a century-old room in Queens College, Cambridge, poring over a Bible and speed-reading huge chunks of Scripture as we tried to find references to the second coming of Christ! At last we found the verses and followed them through for the best part of the night. Can you imagine the thrill?

We had not known, you see, that the One whom our souls loved could return at any moment. "What do you think he'd say if he came back and found us at the ball?" I asked my boyfriend.

"I don't think he'd mind" was the reply. "But why don't we spend the time we have left telling all our friends in that ballroom about this? I'm sure they don't know he's coming again." We spent the rest of the night off the dance floor ministering to groups and individuals. So, my first experience of the impact of that knowledge led me with my friend, now a brother in the Lord, to start to tell other people about it—just as James told other people about it all those years ago. It was an opportunity to warn those who did not know the Lord that they had better get their lives in order. But the few we spoke to who were already believers had a huge blessing in store for them, as did we. One girl had just lost her mother. She was a Christian, but she cried uncontrollably as she shared her loss. We told her about the verses we had just read about Jesus returning and bringing along those who had died with him (1 Thess. 4:13-14), and we watched the comfort, hope, and peace come to her. I learned then that the doctrine of the second coming of Christ can bring warning to the lost and encouragement to persevere to the found.

Our feelings about the second coming of Christ all depend on what is happening in our lives. If we are happy and healthy, we may feel a little ashamed of ourselves, but we may secretly hope that he delays his coming! It is hard to want good times to end, even if our theology tells us there are better times ahead. We are so tied to pleasurable events and relationships in this life that we cling to them. If, on the other hand, we are in the middle of a divorce or battling cancer or watching a child self-destruct, our hearts long for Christ's return as a reprieve and release from the trauma.

James is speaking here to people in the latter

case. The picture he uses to illustrate his point is right out of his listeners' agricultural setting. Farmers wait for the autumn and spring rains. Why? Because they are totally dependent on the Creator God and the forces of nature for the end results. The farmer has done his part but depends on God to bring about the miracle of harvest. God, the One who completes the cycle of nature, has promised that till the end, seed times and harvest will not stop. He wants us to know that the cycle of salvation is just as certain. In fact, it is even more so. One day, the harvest of human souls will be ripe and ready to be gathered safely into heavenly barns. Then the angels will do the reaping, and the Judge will separate the wheat from the chaff. That Judge is Jesus, and as James tells his readers, he is already standing at the door (5:9). In other words, the second coming is about to take place. This information should help those of us who are caught in the misery trap. We have hope of a heavenly escape! It should also jolt those of us who are lazy or complacent into urgent action on the farm! We should be busy plowing, sowing, irrigating—working our heads off for God and his kingdom as we use the good times to prepare our particular field for the better times ahead. We must do our part to multiply the harvest.

What particular quality do we need to exercise while waiting for God to release us from the misery trap? Patience! While we are caught in trauma's grip, whatever shape or size it may be, we need the kind of fortitude to endure that is born of ultimate hope: The patience of the good farmer, a determined faith that perseveres in the belief that one day the trials will be over. Which day this will happen is not our business, but that it will happen, we fully believe.

James turns to the Old Testament for illustrations of how God's best people handled being caught in the misery trap. It is no surprise that the patriarch Job figures as the major example here. "You have heard of Job's perseverance," James says, "and have seen what the Lord finally brought about" (5:11). James was talking to people who knew the Scriptures, but I am not so sure all contemporary Christians would be able to apply his principle without a retelling of the drama of Job. His story, like the stories of Noah and Jonah, are not "musts" anymore, even to churchgoers. Job may be connected in most people's minds to the subject of suffering, but not many of them know much about the circumstances and the final outcome.

Job was an ancient sage, the most famous man of his time. He lived out on the edge of his ancient civilization and pitted his righteousness against the terrorists of his day. God blessed and protected this apparently blameless man, until one day God allowed all sorts of trouble and tragedy to hit him. Job lost his business, his home, his children, his servants, and his land and cattle. (A man's wealth was measured in such things as land and beasts in those days.) Then his health was taken away, too, and he ended up on the garbage heap of his town. The book of Job recounts the man's extraordinary response to all this human misery, his patience and perseverance through the darkest of days. Because they knew this story very well, the people of God came to see Job's patience as a byword.

God finally brought about Job's release from his

misery trap (Job 42:7-16). God restored the man's fortunes and family and bolstered his faith when it faltered. Why? Because, James tells us, "the Lord is full of compassion and mercy" (5:11). God hates to see any of his children caught fast in the misery trap, a lamentable part of a fallen creation. James wants us to think of that little word *finally* and hang on to it. What the Lord did for Job, he will surely do for us. Yes, he will! Our *finally* may be at death, or it might be in this time zone, but we need to persevere in our hope—the inner determination to believe that it will eventually be over.

It is hard to go on believing in God's mercy and grace when life is cruel and hard. We cry out, much like Job, "If God loves me, why is he letting all these terrible things happen to me?" One reason the book of Job gives for human suffering is that our faith may be refined and we may "come forth as gold" (Job 23:10). The quality of our faith is very important and precious to the Lord. So sometimes he allows bad things to happen to us in our fallen state through the course of events in our fallen world, and he does not intervene to stop them. But we are assured that "the Lord has compassion on those who fear him; for he knows how we are formed, he remembers that we are dust" (Ps. 103:13-14). Paul reminds us that God will not test our faith beyond what we can bear (1 Cor. 10:13). There are many verses in the Word that reveal this truth. For example, God, speaking of the Messiah, promises that "a bruised reed he will not break" (Isa. 42:3). Many a time I have clung to that verse, saying over and over, "bruised, but never broken. God said, 'Bruised, but never broken'!"

When you read the wonderful last chapter of Job

and see the Lord help his child out of the terrible misery trap in which he had been so firmly caught, again there is hope. You know what the Lord *finally* brought about, says James. We, too, have God's promise of huge relief! Knowing what God finally brought about for Job gives me the expectation that he will finally bring me relief from today's troubles.

There was a period in my life when that little word *finally* was the fuel for my patience. I was in a painful situation concerning someone I loved very dearly. As I scanned my Bible, I kept coming across promises of God that contained the word *soon*. I did not like being "in transit," so to speak. I wanted my "soon" to become "now," but as we have already seen, our times are in God's hands. He makes everything beautiful by his clock, not ours. Then I read James 5:11, and my heart responded with hope! "God will bring an end to this," I told myself. "Till then I must settle myself to persevere in that hope and trust him to grow patience in my heart as surely as he grows corn in the fields." I had an article due for a magazine and decided to set down my heart's thoughts on this matter. I knew there would be lots of readers who were, like me, on the way to "soon." So I told them about some of the ways I had experienced "The Journey to 'Soon.'" Here is an edited version of what I wrote about:

> One day I was trying to comfort our two-year-old twin grandchildren who were howling because their daddy had kissed them good-bye and was on his way to work.
>
> "He'll be back *soon*," I shouted soothingly. (It is hard to shout soothingly above twin screams, but I did my best.)

My best effort, however, did not alleviate the pain of parting that the twins felt. I realized at once how stupid my attempt had been. What, after all, does *soon* mean to someone that young? When one is a toddler who loves his daddy very much, comfort comes only when "soon" turns into "now."

Listening to the amplified cries of children in distress, I have discovered it is just the same for me. Like my grandchildren, I have real trouble with "soon." Waiting is not my favorite thing to do—especially when I am waiting for something extremely important: a child to be born, a teenager to give me just one little hint she likes belonging to me, or a relative to come to Christ.

But nobody knows how quickly "soon" will be! Except God, that is, and he does not tell us. His knowledge is not withheld to tease, but to test our faith.

Waiting for closure always exposes the caliber of my faith, the intensity of my patience and trust, the shape of my character. And when I am waiting for some particular painful something to be over, there is bound to be some bright, well-meaning saint who "lovingly," and often with ill-conceived satisfaction, comes around to tell me "how much deeper" I will be when it is all finished. I want to scream, "I don't want to be deeper! I want to stay shallow and have the hurt go away soon."

I have learned, however, that what we do with "The Journey to 'Soon'" is vitally important. Waiting does not necessarily mean passivity. Waiting works us over, making us pliable in the Potter's hand. He molds the wet clay (painful waiting nearly always produces lots of moisture) and forms a real grown-up person out of the child in me. So I am learning to take action while I wait.

On a plane not too long ago, I found myself looking forward to a quiet flight, but sitting next to me was a squirmy eight-year-old. Buckling his seat belt like a veteran, he settled back, for all of ninety seconds. He anxiously looked at his watch, and after liftoff I waited for the big question I knew would come! A few more minutes of sighing, gazing out the window, and a lethargic attempt to read a comic book passed before he turned to me and asked, "Are we nearly there?"

"I'm afraid not," I answered apologetically, feeling almost personally responsible for this vital piece of information.

"Maybe there's food on this flight," he suggested hopefully.

"I think there is," I replied.

"That always helps to pass the time," he said.

"What are your favorite foods?" I asked.

I hit a chord and made an eight-year-old friend! We launched into a catalog of our favorites until we finally reached the airport of our destination. My eyes followed him as he was hurried off the plane by a steward. As he disappeared into the terminal, I prayed for him—and for his salvation.

Maybe, I mused, *no one has ever cared for*

his soul. And perhaps if we had arrived sooner, I would not have gotten to know him.

While we are waiting for God to meet our urgent needs, things can be accomplished that only God knows about. Eleven years ago, I watched my mother fight to the death with cancer. I had cried out in agony, "Lord, release her *now!*"

"Soon," he replied. And two days before she died, my mother put her trust in Jesus.

My husband once called to tell me he was extending his evangelistic tour. "But it will soon be over," he said. And his absence until "soon" afforded me the extra time to join a missions team and lead a big fish into the kingdom net!

"Waiting on the Lord" does not mean putting on hold everything else in life until the prayer is answered, the situation redressed, or the nightmare over. "Waiting on the Lord" means cultivating an attitude of trust, casting the bundle of personal cares on him while we busy ourselves with whatever duties we must do. The devil loves to slow us to a dead stop, telling us we need to wait until things are okay again before we serve, teach, preach, or take up our daily responsibilities. He wants to paralyze us with the pain of waiting, so he says, "It will soon be over. Wait until things are back to normal."

This week a new problem has become resident in my life. Like the eight-year-old on the plane, I ask my heavenly Father, "Are we nearly there?"

> I think I hear him saying, "Soon." And that
> gives me hope and strength.

It was hard to write that article but good for my soul, and it reminded me of James's words about patience and perseverance.

So, my friends, know there is an end to being caught in the misery trap. You will see your "soon" turn into "now," and like Job, the "latter part" will be better than "the first" (Job 42:12). The "now" may be in your lifetime, at your death, or when Jesus comes again. We Christians do not know when the Lord will spring us out of our misery traps, but we believe we will be sprung. And so we wait—and work—patiently.

I recently heard about a vicar who lost a child suddenly and very tragically. It is hard for a minister to bear private grief in the public arena, but the man did the best he could. On coming out of a store in the center of his little town, he encountered one of his long-time parishioners. She expressed her condolences and then wanted to know how her pastor was coping with his loss. "Will we be hearing how God is helping you to deal with sorrow this Sunday?" the lady asked. "I'm sure God is helping you to praise him." The minister thought for a long time before he said, "No, the congregation will not be hearing about that this week, but I will *yet* praise him!" That vicar was borrowing words from a psalm by King David.

There are many times in our lives when it seems impossible to praise God, and that is all right. The Lord Jesus himself had such dark periods in his earthly life. But as Christians we know there will be another day—be it here, there, or in the air—

when we will yet praise him! Just knowing that helps. So instead of spending the time pouting, we must try to keep persevering and praying. It makes perfect sense that James bridges his thoughts quite easily from the subject of patience to the subject of prayer.

There is nothing like a good problem to get me praying! James asks, "Are any among you suffering? They should pray" (5:13, NRSV). But why? If, in God's sovereign purposes, he has decided I should stay in a dark time till he determines to get me out of it, why bother praying? Because prayer is so much more than a magic formula for getting us out of our trouble spots. Prayer is our lifeline to heaven. Above all, prayer links us to the God who wants to tell us how the very trouble we find ourselves in can be used to accomplish his ultimate plan, as well as his immediate purposes. He tells us what he wants us to know in a variety of ways: through his Word, through our conscience, through the advice of other believers, or through circumstances.

James uses another illustration from the Old Testament to prove his point. This time he turns to the story of Elijah. "Elijah was a human being like us," he says (5:17, NRSV). Really? We have to stop and think about that! What did he mean by "like us"? The King James Version has it "subject to like passions as we are." Elijah, too, was caught in trouble. He was a wonderful preacher and a mighty prophet, but there was a price on his head. He lived as a fugitive and refugee for three years, coming near to destitution and starvation. He was in really big trouble. If he was "like us," I expect he did not like that very much! Yet Elijah, James says, "prayed earnestly." Before we get around to finding out the content of his prayer, we should think about that word *earnestly*. This describes the caliber of the man's prayer life. Earnestly! James has just told us that "the prayer of the righteous is powerful and effective" (5:16, NRSV). The Phillips version puts it this way: "Tremendous power is made available through a good man's earnest prayer."

James reminds us that Elijah had the power through his prayers to see God make the rain stop and start! As they say, "It's not *what* you know, but *who* you know." Why was this important? Because Ahab, the king of Israel, had fallen away from God and had begun to pray to false gods, and Elijah took this king on! Elijah persevered through his sufferings in hope that "soon" his situation would get better, and meanwhile he cooperated with God's initiatives in the affairs of men. He became God's mouthpiece, risking his own life as he put himself at the disposal of the living God so that his purposes would be worked out on earth. Elijah's problems drove him to prayer that was answered in extraordinary ways. If Elijah had never been in trouble, he would never have seen such wonderful answers from God, and his faith in prayer would never have been fortified.

I find it difficult to pray if I am in trouble, and yet I find it an absolute necessity. I am reminded of the experience of some Korean Christians who testified to the new depth of their prayer lives while being persecuted. They said, "The harder they hit us, the deeper we go."

Again, we must view prayer as more than our cries for personal help. When we are caught fast in the misery trap, it is hard to think of anyone else, much less pray for them. Yet part of our help and healing comes from being busy helping others who are caught in difficult situations right next to us. James talks about people who are sick in body or sick in soul (5:14-15). Sometimes our very affliction can be the bridge over which we can walk into another person's hurting world. James was often in trouble himself, and yet he had time to think about things to do for others who were worse off. Shortly after my mother died, I seemed to meet so many of my friends whose mothers had just died, too. It was good to share our misery as we mourned together, but it was also a healing thing for me to be able to share with my friends the comfort I was getting from God.

In this last chapter of his letter, James talks about people who need their sins healed, not just their sores (like Job) or their sorrows (like Elijah). What sort of sin is James talking about? It appears that he is thinking about the sins of the believer, particularly the sins that cause sisters or brothers in Christ to be estranged from one another. He says, "Therefore confess your sins to each other and pray for each other so that you may be healed" (5:16). Unfortunately, there are such things as sins against each other in the body of Christ. And church fights cause church fissures. We might gossip or falsely accuse each other. We might swear at other Christians, swindle them, and lie, cheat, or steal from them. We might ostracize or criticize, and thereby jeopardize a fellow believer's standing in the Christian community. James notes that these sorts of wounds we inflict on each other need healing!

There is a special sort of misery we suffer if someone who knows the Lord attacks us. Many people have left the church, vowing never to darken the door of a place of worship again, because of a church fight. Perhaps those who know Christ can mete out the worst misery of all! But there is a way out of this trap. We can actually lift the spring from the trapped individual ourselves if we have been at all involved in the problem. James tells us we must first confess our faults to each other and "own" our part of the misery! Then we can pray together about it: "Pray for each other so that you may be healed" (5:16). Healing for broken relationships in Christ is available, but we need to take the initiative through confession and prayer.

There is another sort of misery trap we may be able to do something about. James addresses this right at the end of his letter: "My dear brothers and sisters, if anyone among you wanders away from the truth and is brought back again, you can be sure that the one who brings that person back will save that sinner from death and bring about the forgiveness of many sins" (5:19-20, NLT).

It is a little difficult to figure out just who James is referring to as "that sinner." Is it one of the believers who has backslidden? Or an unbeliever who has been fooled into thinking that white is black and black is white? Fortunately, it is not left to us to judge the matter! God has said, "The Lord does not see as mortals see; they look on the outward appearance, but the Lord looks on the heart" (1 Sam. 16:7, NRSV). One thing we do know is that this is a person who has already been exposed to the truth, but has chosen to "wander" away from it. There is a special misery in this state. When you know what is right but start doing what is wrong, there is a sense of sickness in the soul that is unlike any other misery known to humanity. Spiritual wanderers feel internally rootless, insecure, and vulnerable. Whether folk in this situation were taught the truth but never fully accepted it, or accepted it but strayed a long way from home, they have lost their way and are roaming through life without a sense of purpose or destiny. We need to bring them back to God. We must never be so caught up in our own misery traps that we become callous and indifferent to a sinner's predicament. A life lived in error can lead to spiritual death! A sincere person who is sincerely wrong may end up in hell, as surely as a ship that breaks loose from its moorings may smash on the rocks in a storm.

Sometimes a child brought up in the church will wander away from the church as an adult. One dictionary defines wandering as "turning away from the proper, rational, or sensible course." In spiritual terms, that means going astray morally or intellectually. A young person may say, "Hey, Mom and Dad, I respect you for what you believe, but now I've been at college and have rethought the tenets of my faith. I've discovered it was yours, not mine, and I've decided to believe something else." That person may be caught firmly in the eternal misery trap. The individual who devours the bait of false teaching may well be trapped forever! False teachers are themselves described as "wandering stars, for whom blackest darkness has been reserved forever" (Jude 13).

Yet we who know the Lord's grace and mercy, and who are still "on track" as we orbit around the Son of God, can be used to help the "wandering stars" in our universe find their way back. What a privilege! This is the work to which God has called us—all of us. Perhaps few are called to be teachers, but all are called to be witnesses, which means that any believer can lead a wanderer home. Only God's Holy Spirit can draw a sinner back to himself, yet he has chosen to work through the people who belong to him. They may be happy people, sad people, or hurting people, but because they are his people, they are never suffering too much themselves to be "off duty" when a wanderer crosses their path!

The word wander conjures up images of shepherds, sheep, and sheepfolds. I was once told that a shepherd trains his best sheep to go up an almost-perpendicular mountain and bring down a sheep that has gotten itself into difficulties. Sheep can go where sheep dogs cannot! We can help a wandering sheep because we, too, are sheep in the Lord's fold, and we remember how we were once brought to safety.

There is no greater misery for a sheep than being without a shepherd, and no greater misery for a shepherd than losing even one sheep. What joy there is when the lost sheep comes home! The shepherd lifts that sheep in his arms and carries it to a safe haven. The sheep may be bruised and broken, but it will heal. When a wandering lamb returns to the Good Shepherd, God's joy becomes ours as well. Jesus told us that "there is joy in the presence of the angels of God when one sinner repents" (Luke 15:10, TLB). Says James, "That person who brings [a sinner] back to God will have saved a wandering soul from death, bringing about the forgiveness of his many sins" (5:20, TLB). A multitude of sins are covered, a multitude of miseries are healed, and a multitude of moments are then made available for the "found one" to become a finder of others who are lost.

This year I took a nostalgic trip home to England. A friend had arranged for the girl (now a lady in her sixties!) who had led me to Christ to meet me while I was on a speaking tour. It had been a long time since Janet had smiled at me across the large ward in Addenbrooks Hospital in Cambridge. A lot had happened to both of us. She had gone on to be a medical missionary in Africa and found herself in the middle of a tribal war in the most horrendous conditions. I had met and married Stuart, a banker who subsequently quit the business world and went into the ministry. She and I had renewed contact by mail a few years previous to this meeting, but now—after nearly forty years—we were to see each other face to face and spend the night together in Cambridge, the very place where she had led me to the Lord.

Before Janet arrived, I went to the old hospital where she had, in the words of James, turned this sinner from her error, saved her from death, and covered over a multitude of sins. I took a picture of the building where it had happened and returned to our rendezvous. Janet arrived at dinnertime, and at first we stood and looked at each other, not knowing quite what to say. That state of affairs did not last long, however; all evening and way through the night, we caught up on forty years of loving and serving Jesus. Somewhere along the line, I thanked Janet for her courage in facing me with the truth and being the means of my conversion. She thanked me for going on with the Lord and most of all for putting into practice all she had taught me about leading others to the Christ who had died for me and had lived in my heart all these years. The next day we said good-bye. We held hands and prayed together that we would be faithful to the Lord and to each other. Then Janet looked at me and quoted the apostle John: "I have no greater joy than to hear that my children are walking in the truth" (3 John 4). I knew what she meant. There is indeed no greater joy!

Perhaps you have read to the end of James's letter and are wondering if you have been turned from the error of your ways. If you are wandering, how can you know? Do you believe "the truth"? The truth about what? *First*, the truth about God—that he is holy and that nothing sinful can abide in his presence. *Second*, the truth about yourself—that you are sinful and cannot live in his presence without being forgiven. *Third*, the truth about Jesus Christ—that God was in his Son reconciling the world to himself. That "world" means all the people in it, which means you and me. *Fourth*, the truth about the cross—that the Lord died on that cross to bring wanderers like you and me home to himself. We need to thank him personally for doing that for us. *Fifth*, the truth about the Holy Spirit—that he is Christ's other self. When we confess our sins and turn away from them and invite his Holy Spirit into our lives, the Lord will come in and forgive us. He will cleanse us and live within us to keep us from wandering away from the path of righteousness ever again.

If you believe all this and have received the Holy Spirit by inviting Jesus to come into your life, and you are living in obedience to his Word, you have not wandered. You have turned from the error of your ways. But if you have strayed from "the truth" and need to come back to God, you need some help. A prayer of faith can save you. James said so. Let me pray for you a prayer that Janet prayed years ago for me. If you wish, you can make these words your very own:

> Lord Jesus, I admit I have known about you all my life, but I have not known you personally. I must say in all honesty, I have wandered far away from my religious roots and have been living according to other rules and rituals that have nothing to do with Christianity. I am sorry. I repent. I need you, Lord. I want you, Lord. I now receive you into my life. Amen.

If you echoed that prayer in all sincerity, your many sins are covered over, and you have been saved from spiritual death.

One of the things I thanked Janet for on that reunion night was the assurance she had given me that my sins had been forgiven. I had wondered about that—with my new acute consciousness of my wayward heart and soul. I remember her turning me to Scripture and making me read the words for myself, so I would be able to call on them when I began to doubt and she was not there to help me. I remember the verse that says, "As far as the east is from the west, so far has he removed our transgressions [sins] from us" (Ps. 103:12). "How far is the east from the west, Jill?" Janet had asked me. "A long, long way," I had answered softly. I remember her showing me another reference: Micah 7:18-19. As I read that God would cast our sins "into the depths of the sea," Janet said with a grin,

"And he has put up a sign—*no fishing!*" My sins were covered because Jesus Christ poured out his life and covered them. There was no one else big enough, holy enough, and loving enough who could do that for me! It took a cross and a grave to procure the forgiveness of my sins. I needed only to turn from those sins and reach for my Savior.

What joy and gratitude I felt after I prayed with Janet and she told me that Christ was now in my life! If you have felt in your heart the prayer you just read, he is in your life, too! The Lord Jesus is now within you—to bless you, keep you, lift you up when you are down, encourage you when you are depressed, empower you when you are weak, and give your days purpose and meaning. He brings a joy that is there deep down when you are caught firmly in life's inevitable misery traps, a peace that passes all understanding when the world is at war with you. Christ is your life, your love, your here-and-now, and your forever! Wait patiently in the expectation that our God of compassion and tender mercy will "finally bring about" even greater wonders for you. Live in the good of the Savior's risen life within you—and "guard your heart, for it is the wellspring of life" (Prov. 4:23).

Study Guide: The Misery Trap
For Personal Growth and/or Group Discussion

1. Consider (or discuss) the following: *5 minutes*

   (a) Why should the thought of the second coming of Jesus Christ help us when we are caught fast in the misery trap?

   (b) When do you get most excited about the expected return of Christ? When you are happy? When you are sad? Have you ever told others about Christ's return? What was their reaction?

2. James uses Job as an illustration of a man caught fast in a misery trap. Read the first and last chapters of Job. What do you learn from these two chapters about: *10 minutes*

   (a) the misery trap
   (b) God
   (c) Job

3. Share a lesson you have learned on the way to "soon."   *5 minutes*

4. Read James 5:16-18. Remember that Elijah was in a misery trap. What did you learn from him about praying in pain?   *5 minutes*

Prayer Time   *10 minutes*

1. Read the last words of James (5:19-20).

(a) If you are a wanderer who needs to be found, spend time in prayer about it.

(b) If you are a wanderer who has been found, thank God for it.

2. Do you need to do more about leading wanderers home? Pray by name for someone who fits this category.

8

To Stand for Truth or Abandon It

The Mystical Trap

If the devil fails to catch us in the "me" trap or any of his other devices, he changes direction and comes at us on our "religious" side. He baits the mystical trap with "creedal cheese." "You need your own creed to live by," he suggests in a soothing tone of voice. (You can almost hear church chimes in the background.) "Why don't you develop the mystical side of your nature and join a group of people who don't tell you what you should believe? Take your pick. There's lots to choose from. All grown-up, educated people know that it doesn't really matter what you believe, so long as you're sincere!" Now *there* is the trap! If you think a little bit about it, you will realize it is not sincerity that will save you. (After all, you could be sincerely wrong!)

So often I hear people say things like "We all need faith." They are not quite sure what we need faith *for* or *in,* but the emphasis is put on the faith—as if it is the amount of faith we have that will make a difference in a given situation. If things are difficult for us, it is not uncommon to have someone tell us, "You just don't have enough faith." What many of these people do not realize, however, is that it is the object of our faith that is key. My husband illustrates this very well. Stuart says, "You can have very little faith in very thick ice and stay nice and dry; or you can have a lot of faith in very thin ice and get very wet!" It is not enough simply to "have faith." We need to ask ourselves, "Faith in what or whom?"

Today's Christian woman is faced with a bewildering array of faith choices, whereas it used to be simply "Which denomination should I join?" Even a few dozen years ago, families that moved to new locations across the USA would seek out a church that they had been brought up in or had belonged to in the past. Baptists would search out a Baptist church, Episcopalians an Episcopal church, and so on. Nowadays the ties are not so binding! To add to the general bewilderment of a church mouse looking for a church home, there are denominations splitting among their own ranks. Within one denomination, different local church bodies may take diametrically opposed stands on biblical issues—something which can lead to huge church fights! Disillusionment over a congregational split in the past can lead to attrition in church attendance in the present. If this has been a family's experience, the temptation is not to even bother linking into a denominational setup in a new community. "If we are going to join a church, let's try something new and different," suggests Dad. All too often, Mom—loosened from familiar surroundings and her Christian heritage—may say, "Yes, let's—something really different!" Then she may offer, "I've found the neatest group of people. They more or less believe like we do. Well, not quite the same, but they do think Jesus is the greatest man that ever lived, and that seems okay. They are a lot more broad-minded than the folks back home!"

Some so-called churches have strayed so far from the Word of God that they are not Christian. And some people who speak of "faith" as important would not even claim any link with a church. Perhaps the women at your work, beauty salon, or sports club have been passing around Tracy Mark's book *The Astrology of Self-Discovery,* and the words "by actively using astrology, we can discover our overall life purpose or life directions" have struck a responsive chord in them. Or someone you know is talking about her newfound "spirit guide," and is telling you how to find yours. There may even be some people in your neighborhood talking about the reincarnation of the soul and encouraging you to see a therapist so you can discover all the people you were in previous lives. In fact, talking over such ideas with someone who ardently supports them, a disillusioned and displaced church mouse may be snared into thinking the "new" ideas make more sense than the old beliefs. "There are some parallels with the Christian faith," she may be tempted to say about the reincarnationists' belief that human souls will reappear on earth in a different body after physical death.

If astrology and reincarnation and New Age thinking are a little far out for some of us, the devil may change his bait and put a big piece of "cult cheese" in the trap. This, too, can come in a variety of shapes, smells, and sizes. He can entice us with a piece of doctrine that seems close to what we believe or what we think we believe, that uses Scripture but takes it out of context. He can even come into our churches through such groups as the Christian Identity Movement (which goes by many names) spreading seeds of hate and racial superiority. Or he can come through cults like "The Way," a group that, in a thirteen-week period introduced almost ten thousand families to its "biblical research" and teachings books (see Walter Martin, *The New Cults*). If "The Way" doesn't work, there are similar groups the devil uses: EST, the Children of God (the Family of Love), the Church of the Living Word, the Theosophical Society. The list goes on and on.

There is a definite longing deep down inside every one of us to believe and to belong, but James tells us in no uncertain terms that it matters greatly *what* we believe and *where* we belong! He talks about real faith and about a reliable object for our faith—a saving faith, a faith in a Savior who will prove to be the only one who can fulfill the hunger for God in the human heart, forgive our sins, and give us eternal life.

The word for faith *(pistis)* occurs fifteen times in James's letter, and Paul talks a lot about it in his letters as well. For example, in Ephesians 2:1-10, Paul tells us what faith in God means and what it will do. He says that faith is a divine gift. Although God gives human beings a generous amount of the stuff, where we put that faith is up to us. And Paul tells us it is faith in God's gracious gift of Jesus that alone saves us. What is more, it is not our determination and good works for God that get us to heaven, but rather his effort and saving work on the cross for us that does it! (Eph. 2:8-9).

Most cult members are fervent recruiters, but this is mainly because they believe their efforts to make converts are linked to their own chance of salvation. On the other hand, the Christian's faith is in God, who wants us to trust him to do what is necessary for us, in us, and through us. We are not to trust ourselves, or any prayer or religious ritual, to do what it takes to get us in right standing with the God whom our sin has offended.

Both Paul and James say that we cannot earn our salvation by "observing the law" (Rom. 3:20-28; see James 2:8-13). Faith in Christ is the only means of being made right with God. When Paul insists that salvation is "not by works" (Eph. 2:9), he means that the most important thing all of us need to do is to evaluate our present belief system—our creed. We must ask ourselves some hard questions: "Do I have faith? In whom? In what? What do I expect the object of my faith to do for me? When and how?"

By way of contrast, James talks about a "dead" faith that cannot do anything for us (2:14-26). A mere intellectual tipping of the hat toward certain truths of the Bible, without trusting in Jesus Christ as our Savior, will not bring us eternal life. "I live by the Sermon on the Mount," insists a friend of mine, "so I'll take my chances on getting to heaven along with the rest of the human race. If God thinks

I've done enough good down here, he'll let me inside the pearly gates when my time comes!" I know that many folk share this woman's sincere belief in her own self-effort to gain favor with God. She is sincere, but still wrong! James tells us that a person is not saved by his or her works or "good life." Rather, to use Martin Luther's words, "A man is justified [declared righteous before God] by faith alone, but not by a faith that is alone. Genuine faith will produce good deeds, but only faith in Christ saves."

I find it the hardest thing in the world to convince pleasant, good-living, respectable people, even some who are churchgoers, that they need the Lord Jesus to forgive their sin so they can get to heaven. First of all, it is very hard for such people to believe they are "sinners." Oh, maybe they admit to having shortcomings, but they feel they really are not too bad—especially when they compare themselves to "So and So," someone who is pushed center stage in each of us by the devil whenever our conscience begins to tell us we are not good enough. "So and So" is invariably worse than we are! He or she provides us with a very good reason to be thoroughly complacent about our lives and not bother ourselves with ideas of sin or salvation.

If, perchance, some biblical truth does get through to the "good-living" people, and they find the Lord, they may have such a strong reaction against their past behavior that they never want to have anything to do with good works again! But James asks, "What good is it, my brothers and sisters, if you say you have faith but do not have works?" (2:14, NRSV). Perhaps James would go to worship with a local church fellowship and find himself sitting next to some self-satisfied Pharisee who had joined the group of believers. The man had heard about Jesus Christ, had been attracted by the church's doctrines, and had been converted. In this man's mind, there was now no need to show God his faith in action. After all, God had delivered him from such religiosity! Someone has described such people as "empty headed, empty handed and empty hearted" (Plummer, *Commentary on James*).

Yes, "empty headed," because those who think that head belief is all that God requires will have nothing to offer the Lord at the final judgment. We are not saved by our deeds, but genuine faith can be expected to produce good works. God has prepared works of service for us to do after we have been "justified" by putting our faith in his Son's work on the cross for us. Each of us will one day stand before the Lord and offer him our life's work—the service we have done for him after being born again in Christ.

Paul speaks of this experience as taking place at "the judgment seat of Christ." Writing to the Corinthians, he used an experience he had had in Corinth to illustrate this teaching. While in that city, Paul had run afoul of the authorities and had been hauled up in front of the Roman proconsul at "the judgment seat," or *bema* (court tribunal). Here he was judged and his sentence was decided. Any Christians who witnessed this event in the life of the apostle Paul would have a vivid picture in their mind when they received Paul's letter and learned, "For all of us must appear before the judgment seat of Christ, so that each may receive recompense for what has been done in the body, whether good or evil" (2 Cor. 5:10, NRSV). It is hoped that on that great and dreadful day when our works for Jesus are examined, we will have much of great value to offer God—that we will lay golden faith and silver service at the feet of our Savior (1 Cor. 3:12-15). Years ago I read this poem by an unknown author:

> When I stand at the Judgment Seat of Christ,
> and he shows me his plan for me—
> The plan of my life as it might have been,
> had he had his way—and I see
> How I blocked him here, and checked him there,
> and would not yield my will,
> Shall I see grief in my Savior's eyes?
> grief, though he loves me still?
> He would have me rich, but I stand here poor,
> stripped of all but his grace—
> While my memory runs like a hunted thing,
> down the paths I can't retrace.
> Then my desolate heart will well nigh break
> with tears that I cannot shed.
> I'll cover my face with my empty hands
> and bow my uncrowned head.
> "Now, Lord of the life that's left to me,
> I yield it to thy hand.
> Take me, make me, mold me,
> to the pattern thou hast planned."

One day I will stand before the judgment seat of my Lord Jesus, and I do not want to have empty hands, a desolate heart, and an uncrowned head. Do you?

"Empty headed, empty handed, and empty hearted." It follows quite naturally that if we are "empty headed" about our faith, we will be "empty handed" when we face God. Meanwhile, we will be "empty hearted" right here and now. Without a sacrificial love pulsing within us making us determined to serve—to do or die for God, his kingdom, and his people—there will be little passion in our faith.

There are a lot of reasons why our lives lack spiritual passion. One of them can be that we are not serving Jesus with all our heart and strength. Sometimes people ask me, "Jill, how do you keep on doing what you're doing? How do you keep enthusiastic and passionate about the Lord and his work?" One of the answers to that question is, "I volunteer a lot!" I have done that since the day Janet Smith led me to Christ and told me to wake up every day of my life "determined to be a blessing." As I have made myself "available," I have discovered there are plenty of people in a lost and hurting world that need blessing. I will never run out of work—good work—God's work!

It has been my joy and practice to say YES to everyone and everything I possibly can. *Yes,* when I am asked to travel and speak. *Yes,* when I am asked to visit a dying person in the hospital. *Yes,* when my grandchildren and their parents need me to serve them. *Yes,* when my husband needs companionship or shirts washed or a loving touch. *Yes,* when World Relief has asked me to visit the starving and speak about their situation. *Yes,* to publishers who have been kind enough over the years to invite me to put my teaching into dozens of books. *Yes,* to the women of my church who ask me to set up and run a complex women's ministry for them. *Yes,* to our fine-arts pastor when musical dramas need writing, producing, and directing for our fellowship. Saying YES keeps my spiritual passion at full force, and I have found great joy in serving Jesus—passionate joy! My heart is full.

A true woman of God has a renewed mind, hands full of God's Spirit-directed work, a heart on fire for the God she loves to distraction. Her heart sings in praise, "I love you for first loving me, Lord. Now put my faith to work and help me to do what you've created me to do!" Paul said, "For we are God's workmanship, created in Christ Jesus to do good works, which God prepared in advance for us to do" (Eph. 2:10). The word *workmanship* has the idea of a "work of art." As far as God is concerned, we are his state-of-the-art masterpieces, created in his lovingkindness for a divine reason. By fulfilling his purposes on earth, we find all our desires met. As one Bible commentary puts it, "James doesn't ask for faith plus works, but for faith at work."

Just as emphatically as Paul tells us that we are saved by faith, not by good works, James argues that righteous action is evidence of genuine faith, for we are saved to do the good things God has readied us to do for him and his kingdom—the other side of conversion. Yet many Christians have no clue as to what they are supposed to be doing, what that divine purpose is. Fearing that "doing" will be interpreted as a trust in good works for salvation, some opt for no works! It is a concern of James that we get unconfused and begin to show a faith that is productive. Faith at work is a magnet for people looking for someone to love and care for them. Once people are drawn our way by our kind and loving actions, an articulation of our faith in Christ can prove a powerful means of evangelism for them.

To illustrate his point, James uses two biblical characters as examples. He says first that "Abraham believed God," who credited it (his faith, not his works) to him as "righteousness" (2:23). After Abraham put his trust in God, he demonstrated his faith by action. He obeyed God and offered up his son Isaac. Paul says that "the only thing that counts is faith expressing itself through love" (Gal. 5:6). Faith that saves produces deeds of love. James describes Abraham as a "friend" of God, with the words implying not only companionship, but love on a personal level.

Before I knew the Lord, the only things I did for anyone were things for those closest to me. (I must confess I did not do too many of those either!) I did express love to my mother by my actions when I was helping in the kitchen at mealtimes, but it was never my favorite thing to do. I loved my mom, however, and knew that her faithfulness to me could be counted on. So I did my good work to show her I loved and appreciated her. I never helped in the kitchen to win points or to get her to love or accept me. My works expressed my faith in her and my love for her. It was only after I had come to a living faith in God that I began to volunteer to help those who needed help outside family boundaries.

Perhaps you also are willing to extend yourself as a volunteer but do not know how to find where you are needed. You may say, "I've been a member of my church for years and years, but no one has ever called me up and invited me to serve." Then do not wait any longer! Pick up that phone you have been waiting to answer all this time and ask, "What needs doing?" Tell whoever is on the other end of the line, "I'll have a go at it. I'll do it." If you call up your pastor, hospital, PTA board, local retirement home, or soup kitchen and ask that very simple question, "How can I help you?" you will never be idle or bored again!

Of course, all this is a little risky. What if your offer is rejected? What if you cannot do what needs doing? What if you fail? Because of the "what ifs," many of us never get around to the good works prepared by God for us to do. But *what if* God gives you wisdom and strength beyond your own (which he promises to all those who do his will and work)? And *what if* the risk you take drives you to depend on him and you find him faithful? And that is what will happen! We all need to come to the time in life when we burn our bridges behind us, throw in our lot with the people of God, and take the risks God wants us to take in his name for the sake of others.

The second biblical character James uses as an example of faith at work is a rather surprising example—a prostitute named Rahab, who took a great risk for the people of God. Her faith saved her and resulted in her doing God's work and will. This Old Testament story (Josh. 2:1-22) tells how Joshua, the commander-in-chief of Israel's army, had sent out two spies to Caanan to try to find out how strong was the enemy city of Jericho. *What are we up against?* Joshua wondered. God had told him to move into Caanan and possess the land, and the very first fortified city they encountered was mighty Jericho. Rahab lived in one of the houses built right inside the walls of that city. Though a lady of ill repute, she received Joshua's spies and bravely hid them when the soldiers of Jericho came looking for them. Rahab risked her life to save theirs. When the soldiers hammered on her door, demanding that the men be delivered (they had been seen going into her house), she sent the soldiers off in the wrong direction to look for them. James does not condone Rahab's occupation, but he does commend her faith, which she demonstrated by helping the spies escape (2:15). Her good work is also mentioned elsewhere in the New Testament (Heb. 11:31).

For Rahab and Abraham, and for all of us, unless faith in the one true God results in practical results for good, it is not genuine faith. As William Barclay puts it, "Unless Abraham had had faith, he would never have answered the summons of God. Unless Rahab had had faith, she would never have taken the risk of identifying her future with the fortunes of Israel. And yet, unless Abraham had been prepared to obey God to the uttermost, his faith would have been unreal; and unless Rahab had been prepared to risk all to help the spies, her faith would have been useless" *(The Letters of James and Peter,* Westminster Press, 1976).

James sheds more light on his point about faith at work when he acknowledges that even demons believe in the one and only true God—"so strongly that they tremble in terror!" (2:19, TLB). Demons are capable of intellectual assent to the truth about God, but they do not possess a faith that saves or serves.

> Jesus frequently encountered persons possessed by demons, but they always recognized deity and spoke respectfully (Matt. 8:29; Mark 1:24; 5:7; Luke 8:28; Acts 16:17; 19:15). Yet it was clear that the intellectual understanding of God held by demons produced in them only the fear of certain doom,

not the fruit of repentance toward God and trust in Jesus Christ. The problem was not that their faith was insincere. On the contrary, they believed so completely in the coming doom that God has promised that they shuddered at the prospect. It is clear, therefore, that mere intellectual assent to the fact of God's oneness, as represented in the faithful reciting of the Shema, was not sufficient to save anyone. True faith must go beyond this to the point of trust and acceptance. (Homer Kent, *Faith that Works,* Baker, 1986, p. 97).

Although demons are incapable of good works—since they personify evil, and evil serves only itself—we who are "created in God's image" can choose to express our beliefs in behavior that blesses others and ourselves and brings glory to the One we have come to love and serve. This is a point at which the devil panics, so he tries to direct our attention away from the one and only God. Having lost that battle, he next tries to convince us to *believe* only and not put our faith to good use. This way, he can catch unwary Christians in his mystical trap. If Satan can get us to concentrate all our energies on being "spiritually-minded," we will have nothing to offer his most dreaded and hated opponent at the end of the day. If even this tactic does not work, he tries to make us work our heads off doing "good things" until we become either totally exhausted or conceited about all we are doing for God. Satan has won if we fall into the trap of trying to work our way to heaven (along with half the human race) when we have already been delivered from such fruitless endeavors!

In any well-balanced life, there must be faith *and* deeds. James reminds us that there are not two classes of Christians—some who spend all their time on their knees, secluded in constant devotion to God, and others who work for God till they drop! I especially like William Barclay's illustration of this truth in his Bible commentary *The Letters of James and Peter*. He tells this story about Martin Luther:

> It is said that Martin Luther was close friends with another monk. The other was as fully persuaded of the necessity of the Reformation as Luther was, so they made an arrangement. Luther would go down into the world and fight the battle there; the other would remain in his cell praying for the success of Luther's labours. But one night the monk had a dream—in it he saw a single reaper engaged in the impossible task of reaping an immense field by himself. The lonely reaper turned his head, and the monk saw his face—the face of Martin Luther. He knew that he must leave his cell and his prayers and go to help. It is, of course, true that there are some who, because of age or bodily weakness, can do nothing other than pray; and their prayers are indeed a strength and a support. But if any normal person thinks that prayer can be a substitute for effort, his prayers are merely a way of escape. Prayer and effort must go hand in hand. In any

well-proportioned life there must be faith and deeds. It is only through deeds that faith can prove and demonstrate itself; and it is only through faith that deeds will be attempted and done. Faith is bound to overflow into action; and action begins only when a man has faith in some great cause or principle which God has presented to him.

So what does all this mean for Christian women in our own generation? It means we must escape the mystical trap and reject the devil's offerings! We must worship God alone as revealed in Christ, of course, but we must also show our faith in works of service that will set our world apart and make people receptive to the message of salvation. The Christian church is replete with stories of men and women who through the ages have shown their faith by their deeds and have at every opportunity explained these deeds of faith to anyone who would listen.

Now it is our turn to bring others to Christ, and we can look to history for encouragement. Take Mary Mitchell Slessor, for instance. Mary was a Scottish lass who came to a true and living faith in Christ. In 1876, at the age of twenty-six, she went to Calabar (present-day Nigeria) to spend her life in pioneer missionary work. This involved works of service that would put all of us to shame! Or think of Ann Hasseltine Judson, married to the famous missionary Adoniram Judson (the first American missionary). Together this couple went to India and later to Burma, where they faced incredible hardships for the cause of Christ. At one time Ann's husband was thrown into a Burmese death prison and was there for two long and dreadful years. Ann wrote lucidly and movingly of her struggles at that time and of her good works on behalf of the people she loved and served and for whom she had left all the world's comforts.

In *Daughters of the Church* (Zondervan, 1987), Ruth Tucker says about Ann Judson, "Her heart went out specifically to the women who suffered child marriages, endured female infanticide, and were addressed by their husbands as 'my servant' or 'my dog' and allowed only to eat their spouse's scraps when he was done with his meal. Ann worked tirelessly to 'ameliorate the situation, to instruct, to enlighten and save females in the Eastern world.'" Surely here are two shining missionary examples of faith at work! Ann Judson's heartbeat was to change the world through God's plan for her. Speaking of the great love God gave her for these women, she says, "Shall we suffer minds like theirs to lie dormant—to wither in ignorance and delusion—to grope their way to eternal ruin without an effort on our part to raise, to refine, to elevate, and point to that Saviour who has died equally for them as for us?" Women like Mary Slessor and Ann Judson had saving faith. How do we know? Because of its concrete expression—its outworking in a hurting world.

But perhaps you do not see yourself as a missionary in far-away places. Maybe you cannot relate to the Mary Slessors and Ann Judsons of this world. Then consider Catherine Booth, wife of William Booth, founder of the Salvation Army. There you have an example in the western world of the unity of faith and works. As Ruth Tucker relates, "Catherine had read the Bible through eight times by the time she was twelve years of age and knew and loved the Lord all her young years. Co-founder of the Salvation Army with her husband William, she put her faith to work in the West End of London with the 'up and outers' and in the East End with the 'down and outers.' She got busy reclaiming women and especially teenagers from lives of prostitution, and became active in the temperance movement establishing rescue missions. Catherine worked out her faith by forming churches among some who were called 'human refuse' by other churches who regarded them with blank despair" *(Daughters of the Church).*

Catherine trained other women workers, seven of whom were sent off to begin the work of the Salvation Army in America. Tucker comments, "There was no condescending to them on account of their sex, as is illustrated in the farewell prayer offered by an Army officer: 'Lord, these ladies are going to America to preach the gospel. If they are fully given up to Thee, be with them and bless them and grant them success. But if they are not faithful, drown 'em, Lord, drown 'em!' They did succeed, and they served as an example, along with many others, that prompted William Booth to say, 'My best men are women.'"

Have you ever wondered about the children of such intrepid faith-workers? I have. It intrigued me, therefore, to read Catherine Booth's comment when questioned about her parenting. "How have you managed to get your children converted so early?" she was asked. She replied, "I have been beforehand with the devil. I have not allowed my children to become pre-occupied with the things of the world before I have got the seed of the kingdom well in."

I do not have to look far from home to find an example of how powerful an impact a living faith can have on our children. Not many years ago, a refugee family from Thailand arrived in Milwaukee. One of our employees at that time, a former bank manager and recovering alcoholic, took this family of six into his home. John and his own family moved upstairs and gave the newcomers (who could speak no English) the entire downstairs. John had recently recommitted his life to the Lord, and together with his wife, Shirley, he began to work with the steady stream of displaced people who came to our city. These two showed others their faith by their works, and it was no surprise to anyone to see John and Shirley eventually end up in Asia as missionaries. And what of their kids? How did they take to giving over half of their house to strangers? Luke now serves in his father's place at church. Daughter Anna lives on the mission field with her parents and has a heart full of love for Asia! John, Jr., married a refugee from Laos and is presently in the United States Marine Corps. Lisa is at this time working with abused children in Lexington, Kentucky. These children discovered, along with their parents, that a faith that works is a working faith, and they want no less for themselves!

Like Catherine Booth, John and Shirley could well testify to the importance of our planting "the seed of the kingdom" early in a child's life and nurturing its growth through our own lively, working faith. As parents we must look to our own faith lives and make sure we have things in balance. Our children are watching us! They see us on Sunday,

but they see us on Monday, too. They hear us singing hymns about serving Jesus, but all too often
they see us serving mainly ourselves.

What do you do for vacations? Have you ever
taken the family to Mexico to help build a clinic,
or ventured to an urban area closer to your home
to put up housing for poor families? Do you put
your money where your mouth is? Children see,
and children know what is important to us. It is no
surprise to me to meet children of missionaries
back on the field or engaged in Christian service at
home. I smile when I bump into a wealthy young
businessman investing his time, talents, and funds
in helping relief agencies show refugees how to
start small businesses, and then find out that his
dad was an accountant for a mission in the Philip-
pines. A faith that works is like measles—it is catching! In fact, a faith that does not show itself in
works of service holds little credibility with the
youth of today. Our youngsters see through piety
that never gets its hands dirty for the poor or disenfranchised. They are not interested enough to investigate a faith that has no faith in what faith can
do. They desperately need to see a faith that makes
a difference in the world because it furthers the
purposes of a living, dynamic, one and only God.

Whenever our extended family gathers for vacation, we get out the scrapbooks, the photos, and
the slides, and we talk well past midnight about
the works of God all of us have experienced in our
lives. We are blessed to have such a rich Christian
heritage. Stuart and I often tell stories about the
youth work we were involved with in Liverpool and
Manchester. Our own children still remember those
days. They remember many of those street kids be-

ing converted. David (our oldest) may chip in to remind us about a character called "Grotty Bob," who was a drug dealer in Manchester. Stuart was working among the unchurched young people in the cities at that time and brought him home to stay with us awhile. David, then six, still remembers Grotty Bob's conversion and the dramatic change in his life and behavior. Our son had been part of it all—starting with giving up his own bed so Grotty Bob could sleep comfortably for a change. We all learned about life in another culture through that experience, especially that it is very hard living by your wits on the streets!

It was Stuart's faith in a God who has the power to transform that nudged him into bringing that lost young man into our home. Next, good works were needed to look after Bob's mind and body and care for his soul. It was not our preaching so much as our "practicing" that finally made the difference. That young man seemed overwhelmed that we would open our home to him, share our beds, bathroom, meals, and family, wash his clothes, listen to his woes, pray for him every day, and *love* him into the kingdom. Bob did not forget that, and neither did young David. Perhaps that is the reason our son serves with us on staff at Elmbrook Church in the area of Assimilation—caring for the many outsiders, visitors, and strangers who come to our gates. The apple does not fall far from the tree!

Greg, our daughter Judy's husband, talks about the Bibles his family packaged up years ago to send to a previously unreached group of people overseas. A short time ago on a business trip to New York, he met some people from that country. (The wife of one of the men was a princess!) How excited Greg was to tell them he had sent Bibles to their country as a child and why. Both Judy and Greg, now leaders in their church, spend time helping such organizations as Habitat for Humanity as well.

Debbie, David's wife, takes a turn relating the excitement of growing up as a pastor's kid, sharing her busy parents with families in need in poor rural areas. Libby, our son Pete's wife, adds story after story of the endless stream of broken, bruised, and battered people taken into her family's home in her growing years. There they found practical help and healing through Christ. It is no wonder all our children and their partners serve God today. Thank the Lord that with all our faults, we parents were able to practice enough faith-in-action to make our own kids hunger for the same reality for themselves and their children. The heritage is passed along! The very best thing we can do for future generations is to show them our faith by our works.

One modern gospel song by Jon Mohr captures this idea very well:

> Oh, may all that come behind us find us faithful,
> May the fire of our devotion light their way.
> May the footsteps that we leave, lead them to
>   believe,
> And the lives we lead inspire them to obey.
> Oh, may all that come behind us find us faithful.

If we are to show this kind of faithfulness, we must not let Satan lure us into the mystical trap! Only God can offer the gift of salvation. Jesus Christ said, "I am the way and the truth and the life. No one comes to the Father except through me" (John

14:6). The apostle Peter stated clearly enough, "There is no other name under heaven given among mortals by which we must be saved" (Acts 4:12, NRSV). And the story does not stop with our receiving salvation—as James puts it, we are saved to serve, blessed to be a blessing! "I will show you my faith by what I do," he says. At Christ's coming may we be found doing the same!

Study Guide: The Mystical Trap

For Personal Growth and/or Group Discussion

1. Review time   *10 minutes*

    (a) Read James 2:14-25.
    (b) Which verse particularly struck you? Why?

2. Story time   *5 minutes*

    (a) Give an historical example of a faith/works life.
    (b) Give a modern-day example of such a life.

3. Read Ephesians 2:1-10. Then go through each verse and put it in your own words. The result will be a summary of what faith in God is and does, according to Paul.   *10 minutes*

Prayer Time   *5 minutes*

1. Pray for each other, that your world will see your faith in action.

2. Pray for people who need some "good works" done for them.

3. Pray for Christian compassionate relief agencies around the world.